BLEST ARE WE

Series Authors
Rev. Richard N. Fragomeni, Ph.D.
Maureen Gallagher, Ph.D.
Jeannine Goggin, M.P.S.
Michael P. Horan, Ph.D.

Scripture Co-editor and Consultant
Maria Pascuzzi, SSL, S.T.D.

Multicultural Consultant
Angela Erevia, MCDP, M.R.E.

The Ad Hoc Committee to Oversee the Use of the Catechism, United States Conference of Catholic Bishops, has found this catechetical series, copyright 2002, to be in conformity with the Catechism of the Catholic Church.

SILVER BURDETT GINN RELIGION
A SCOTT FORESMAN IMPRINT
PARSIPPANY, NJ

Contributing Writer
Janie Gustafson, Ph.D.

Contributing Authors
Family Time: Steve and Kathy Beirne
We Care: Richard Reichert, M.A.
Feasts and Seasons: Marianne K. Lenihan
Our Catholic Heritage: Patricia Enwright
Unit Organizers and Reviews: Joyce A. Crider

Advisory Board
William C. Allegri, M.A., Patricia M. Feeley, SSJ,
M.A., Edmund F. Gordon, Patricia A. Hoffmann, Cris
V. Villapando, D.Min.

Consultants
Margaret J. Borders, M.R.S., Kelly O'Lague Dulka,
M.S.W., Diane Hardick, M.A., Debra Schurko, Linda
S. Tonelli, M.Ed., Joy Villotti-Biedrzycki

Music Advisor
GIA Publications: Michael A. Cymbala, Alec Harris,
Robert W. Piercy

Nihil Obstat
M. Kathleen Flanagan, S.C., Ph.D.
Ellen Joyce, S.C., Ph.D.
Censors Librorum

Imprimatur
✠Most Reverend Frank J. Rodimer
Bishop of Paterson
January 26, 2001

The *nihil obstat* and *imprimatur* are official declarations that a book
or pamphlet is free of doctrinal and moral error. No implication is
contained therein that those who have granted the *nihil obstat* and
imprimatur agree with the contents, opinions, or statements expressed.

Acknowledgments
Excerpts from *The New American Bible* © 1970 by the Confraternity
of Christian Doctrine, Washington, DC, including the revised *New
Testament* © 1986 by the Confraternity of Christian Doctrine,
Washington, DC, used with permission. All rights reserved.

All adaptations of Scripture are based on *The New American Bible* ©
1970 and 1986.

Excerpts from the English translation of the *Rite of Baptism for
Children* © 1969, International Committee on English in the Liturgy,
Inc. (ICEL); excerpts from the English translation of the *Rite of
Penance* © 1974, ICEL; excerpts from the English translation of
Eucharistic Prayers for Masses with Children © 1975, ICEL; excerpts
from the English translation of *The Roman Missal*, Second Edition ©
1985, ICEL. All rights reserved.

Music selections copyrighted and/or administered by GIA Publications
are used with permission of GIA Publications, Inc., 7404 So. Mason
Avenue, Chicago, IL 60638-9927. Please refer to songs for specific
copyright dates and information.

"Thumb Prayer" adapted from *Catechist* magazine. © Page McKean
Zyromski, Contributing Editor.

In Appreciation: Blessed Kateri Church, Sparta, NJ; Blessed
Sacrament Church, Newark, NJ; Church of the Assumption,
Morristown, NJ; Our Lady of Mercy Church, Whippany, NJ; Our Lady
of the Lake Church, Sparta, NJ; Saint Ann's Church, Parsippany, NJ;
Saint Joseph's Church, Croton Falls, NY; Saint Peter the Apostle
Church, Parsippany, NJ; Saint Thomas More Church, Convent Station,
NJ; OCP Publications, Portland, OR; GIA Publications, Inc., Chicago, IL;
WLP Publications, Schiller Park, IL

Credits
DESIGN: Lusignan Design and Scott Foresman
COVER: Gene Plaisted, OSC/The Crosiers
LET US PRAY ART: Maria Jimenez
SCRIPTURE ART: Diane Paterson

ALL OTHER ART: 19 Nan Brooks; 23 Diana Magnuson; 27 Lyn
Martin; 34 Masami Miyamoto; 35 Laura Huliska-Beith; 39 Melinda
Levine; 43 Lyn Martin; 47, 48 Marion Eldridge; 55 Stephen
Carpenter; 55 George Ulrich; 58 Dorothy Stott; 63 Randy Chewning;
66, 67 Morella Fuenmayor; 75 Jean & Mou-sien Tseng; 79 Paige
Billin-Frye; 83 Laura Huliska-Beith; 87 Jean & Mou-sien Tseng;
88 Shelley Dieterichs; 89 Stephen Carpenter; 90 Shelley Dieterichs;
95 Judy Stead; 99 Tom Sperling; 111 George Hamblin; 111 George
Hamblin 114 Dorothy Stott; 114 Roman Dunets; 119 George
Hamblin; 123 Linda Howard Bittner; 123 Patti Greene; 127 Shelley
Dieterichs; 128 Jean & Mou-sien Tseng; 129 Marion Eldridge;
138 Dorothy Stott; 138 Roman Dunets; 143 Randy Chewning;
147 David Austin Clar; 151 Randy Chewning; 155 Lauren Cryan;
159 Randy Chewning; 163 Pat Hoggan; 167 Marion Eldridge;
169, 170 Shelley Dieterichs; 178 Jill Dubin; 183 Morella
Fuenmayor; 186 Jane Robbins; 187 Gregg Valley; 191 Donna
Perrone; 195 Tom Sperling; 195 Pat Hoggan; 203 Sandy
Rabinowitz; 206 Marcie Hawthorne; 207, 208 Shelley Dieterichs;
213 Lyn Martin; 214 Linda Weller; 215 Randy Chewning;
217 Kathleen Kuchera; 221 Morella Fuenmayor; 225 Cindy
Rosenheim; 226, 227 Diane Paterson; 228 Dorothy Stott; 233 Tom
Sperling; 268 Elizabeth Wolf

PHOTOS: 11 Jim Whitmer; 14 James L. Shaffer; 21 Bill and Peggy
Wittman © W.P. Wittman; 22 National Gallery, London/Photograph by
Erich Lessing/Art Resource, NY; 28 James L. Shaffer; 31 Vince
Streano/Corbis; 31 David J. Sams/Stock Boston; 31 Myrleen
Ferguson/PhotoEdit; 36 Donald Nausbaum/Stone; 44 Pablo
Coral/Corbis; 51 Z. Radovan, Jerusalem; 54 Hermitage Museum,
St. Petersburg, Russia/Bridgeman Art Library, London/SuperStock;
60 Tim Brown/Stone; 62 Corbis Sygma; 68 Jim Whitmer;
68 PhotoDisc; 70 Everett Collection, Inc.; 74 Jim Whitmer; 76 Adam
Woolfitt/Woodfin Camp & Associates/PhotoQuest; 78 Everett
Collection, Inc.; 84 CLEO; 91 Barry Searle/©Sonia Halliday
Photographs; 91 Editorial Development Associates; 94 Newberry
Library, Chicago/SuperStock; 100 Robert Fried Photography;
102 Macduff Everton/Corbis; 103 Lawrence Migdale/Stone;
106 Stephen McBrady/PhotoEdit; 108 Paul Conklin/PhotoEdit;
110 Catholic News Service; 116 Bettmann/Corbis; 116 Danilo G.
Donadoni/Bruce Coleman Inc.; 118 Gene Plaisted, OSC/The
Crosiers; 122 Index Stock Imagery; 124 Earth Imaging/Stone;
125 Patrick Johns/Corbis; 126 Milt & Joan Mann/Cameramann
International, Ltd.; 131 Z. Radovan, Jerusalem; 131 © Tony
Freeman/PhotoEdit/PictureQuest; 140 Tony Freeman/PhotoEdit;
141 Felicia Martinez/PhotoEdit; 142 Bettmann/Corbis; 150 Catholic
News Service; 157 Milt & Joan Mann/Cameramann International,
Ltd.; 158 Scala/Art Resource, NY; 164 John Gerlach/TOM STACK &
ASSOCIATES; 164 C.P. George/Visuals Unlimited; 171 David
Lees/Corbis; 171 Michael Newman/PhotoEdit; 174 Rasmussen/Sipa
Press; 175 Catherine Karnow/Woodfin Camp & Associates;
175 E. Crews/Image Works; 178 Don Smetzer/Stone; 180 Peter
Cade/Stone; 182 Courtesy, Little Sisters of the Poor; 184 Gene
Plaisted, OSC/The Crosiers; 188 Michael Gadomski/Animals
Animals/Earth Scenes; 190 Dick S. Ramsay Fund/Brooklyn Museum;
194 Lori Grinker/Contact Press Images; 194 Charles Caratini/Corbis
Sygma; 194 Lawrence Migdale/Stock, Boston/PictureQuest;
194 Daemmrich Photography; 196 David Tejada/Stone; 198 Richard
Nowitz ©Richard T. Nowitz; 202 Robert Brenner/PhotoEdit;
202 Myrleen Cate/PhotoEdit; 204 Milt & Joan Mann/Cameramann
International, Ltd.; 205 Stuart Cohen/Image Works; 211, 216 Ariel
Skelley/Stock Market; 218 Jack Kurtz/Impact Visuals;
220 SuperStock; 222 James L. Shaffer; 224 Alinari/Regione
Umbria/Art Resource, NY; 230 Flip Schulke/Corbis; 231 The
Pierpont Morgan Library/Art Resource, NY; 235, 237, 239 Bill and
Peggy Wittman © W.P. Wittman; 239 Bob Daemmrich/Image Works;
248 Myrleen Ferguson/PhotoEdit; 248 The Pierpont Morgan
Library/Art Resource, NY; 249 Jose L. Pelaez/Stock Market;
255 Myrleen Ferguson/PhotoEdit; 256 Bob Daemmrich/Stock,
Boston/PictureQuest

ALL OTHER PHOTOS: Scott Foresman and Pearson Learning

7 8 9 10 – V003 – 09 08 07 06 05 04

Our Commitment Prayer

_____

- -

Name _____

Leader: God, our Creator, you take good care of everything that you have made.

All: We will help care for the gifts of creation.

Leader: God, our Father, the stories in the Bible tell us about Jesus' life and teachings.

All: We will listen carefully to your holy word.

Leader: Merciful God, you are always ready to forgive us. Your love for us is everlasting.

All: We will be sorry when we choose to do wrong. We will ask for your forgiveness.

Leader: Loving God, you sent your Son, Jesus, into the world to be our Savior.

All: We will remember Jesus' life, death, and Resurrection each time we celebrate the Eucharist.

Leader: God, you sent the Holy Spirit to help and guide the members of the Catholic Church.

All: We will ask the Holy Spirit for the gifts we need to serve others.

CONTENTS

Blest Are We

Words and Music by David Haas
Spanish translation by Ronald F. Krisman

REFRAIN

Blest are we, ho - ly chil - dren of light— are— we!_____
¡Ben-de-ci - dos, so - mos san - tos hi - jos de la luz!

Blest are we, cho - sen peo - ple of God!_____
¡Ben-de-ci - dos y e - le - gi - dos por Dios!_____

Blest are we, God has plans___ for you and me!_____
¡Ben-de-ci - dos, Dios nos quie - re - ser cual Je - sús!

Blest___ are we!___ We are the chil - dren of God!_____
¡Ben - de-ci - dos, so - mos los hi - os de Dios!_____

VERSE

1. For our world,___ each sis - ter and broth - er:
1. Por el - mun - do, por to - dos sus pue - blos:

We___ are called,___ called___ to serve!___
¡So - mos lla - ma - dos pa - ra ser - vir!___

We are here to love___ one an - oth - er:
Nos a - me - mos los u - nos a los o - tros;___

We___ are called, ___ called___ to serve!_____
¡So - mos lla - ma - dos pa - ra ser - vir!___

2. For the poor, the meek and the lowly:
   We are called, called to serve!
   For the weak, the sick and the hungry:
   We are called, called to serve!

2. Por los pobres, los mansos y humildes:
   ¡Somos llamados paraservir!
   Por los enfermos, ham brientos, y débiles:
   ¡Somos llamados paraservir!

3. For all those who yearn for freedom:
   We are called, called to serve!
   For the world, to be God's kingdom:
   We are called, called to serve!

3. Por los que sefren y quieren ser librados:
   ¡Somos llamados paraservir!
   Venga a nosotros el Reino de los Cielos:
   ¡Somos llamados paraservir!

LET US PRAY

Sign of the Cross

In the name of the Father,
and of the Son,
and of the Holy Spirit.
Amen.

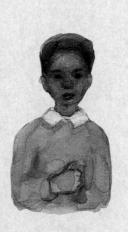

The Lord's Prayer

Our Father,
who art in heaven,
hallowed be thy name;
thy kingdom come;
thy will be done on earth
as it is in heaven.
Give us this day
our daily bread;
and forgive us
our trespasses
as we forgive those
who trespass against us;
and lead us not
into temptation,
but deliver us from evil.
Amen.

Hail Mary

Hail Mary, full of grace,
the Lord is with you.
Blessed are you among
women,
and blessed is the fruit
of your womb, Jesus.
Holy Mary, Mother of God,
pray for us sinners,
now, and at the hour
of our death.
Amen.

Glory Be
to the Father

Glory be to the Father,
and to the Son,
and to the Holy Spirit.
As it was in the
beginning, is now,
and will be forever.
Amen.

Nicene Creed

We believe in one God,
  the Father, the Almighty,
  maker of heaven and earth,
  of all that is seen and unseen.

We believe in one Lord, Jesus Christ,
  the only Son of God,
  eternally begotten of the Father,
  God from God, Light from Light,
  true God from true God,
  begotten, not made, one in Being with the Father.
  Through him all things were made.
  For us men and for our salvation
    he came down from heaven:

by the power of the Holy Spirit
  he was born of the Virgin Mary,
    and became man.

For our sake he was crucified under Pontius Pilate;
  he suffered, died, and was buried.
  On the third day he rose again
    in fulfillment of the Scriptures;
  he ascended into heaven
    and is seated at the right hand of the Father.

He will come again in glory to judge
  the living and the dead,
    and his kingdom will have no end.

We believe in the Holy Spirit, the Lord, the giver of life,
who proceeds from the Father and the Son.
With the Father and the Son he is worshiped and glorified.
He has spoken through the Prophets.
We believe in one holy catholic and apostolic Church.
We acknowledge one baptism for the forgiveness of sins.
We look for the resurrection of the dead,
and the life of the world to come.

Amen.

Prayer to the Holy Spirit

Come, Holy Spirit,
fill the hearts of your faithful
and kindle in them
the fire of your love.
Send forth your Spirit,
and they shall be created;
and you will renew
the face of the earth.
Amen.

Morning Prayer

Loving God, bless the work we do.
Watch over us and guide us in
   school and at home.
Help us realize that everything
   we do gives praise to you.
We make this prayer in
   Jesus' name.
Amen.

Evening Prayer

Parent: May God bless you and
            keep you.
Child: May he guide you in life.
Parent: May he bless you this
            evening.
Child: And keep us in his sight.
Parent: May God be with you,
            (name).
Child: And also with you.
Together: In the name of the Father,
            and of the Son,
            and of the Holy Spirit.
            Amen.

Grace Before Meals

Bless us, O Lord, and these your gifts,
   which we are about to receive
   from your goodness,
   through Christ our Lord.
Amen.

Grace After Meals

We give you thanks for all your gifts,
   almighty God,
   living and reigning
   now and forever.
Amen.

Prayer to My Guardian Angel

Angel of God, my guardian dear,
  to whom God's love commits me here.
Ever this day be at my side
  to light and guard, to rule and guide.
Amen.

My Prayer to Jesus in the Eucharist

_____
_____
_____
_____
_____
_____
_____
_____
_____
_____

Amen.

We Gather as Believers

Our parish church community comes together each week. We give praise and thanks to God and we celebrate our faith.

It is good to give thanks to the Lord, to sing praise to your name, Most High.

Psalm 92:2

King David gave thanks to God through joyful song. We gather in church to sing our praise and thanks to God.

You Have Put On Christ

Music by Howard Hughes

Cantor, then All

You— have— put on Christ, in him you have been bap - tized.

Al - le - lu - ia, al - le - lu - ia.

© 1977, ICEL.

FAMILY TIME

A choice of things to do at home

Our Church Welcomes Us

The chapters in Unit 1 focus on membership in the Catholic Church. This first chapter explains being welcomed into the community of believers and being a small part of something larger.

Plant a vine

Together, plant a vine, such as ivy, in a flowerpot, or buy one already planted. Help your child name the parts of the plant (roots, stems, and leaves) and then realize that these small parts make up the whole plant.

You're welcome!

What relatives and friends have made you feel welcome in their homes? Encourage your child to role-play being a welcomed guest and a welcoming host.

Have a doughnut

Eat some doughnuts or some other round food to remind you that we are all one. The circle is a sign of unity. Talk about how people around the world are part of the Church, the Body of Christ.

✝ A Prayer for the Week

We are blessed, dear Lord, to be part of your Church, the Body of Christ. Help us show that we are happy to be followers of Jesus.
Amen.

FAMILY TIME

Something to Do . . .

On Sunday

Show hospitality to others. As you go into church, greet the people around you and make them feel welcome.

Through the Week

Light a candle for people in your parish who need your prayers. Remember that you and they are part of the Body of Christ.

Visit Our Web Site

 www.blestarewe.com

Something to Think About . . .

Showing Hospitality

Then Levi gave a great banquet for him in his house.
Luke 5:29

Levi, the man in this story who invited Jesus to dinner at his house, welcomed Jesus warmly. He treated him with courtesy and showed him hospitality.

When someone comes to your home as a guest, you try to make that person feel welcome and comfortable. Showing interest in and respect for your guest is what hospitality means. Being a good host in your home shows your child or children how to be hospitable.

Something to Know About . . . Our Heritage

In the early Church the Eucharist was celebrated around a table, usually as a shared meal. During the great persecutions, the Eucharist was often celebrated using the tombs of the martyrs as altar tables.

During the Middle Ages, permanent altars became quite ornate and eventually looked more like monuments than tables for a sacred meal.

Inspired by the Second Vatican Council, twentieth-century reforms in the liturgy called for the celebrant to face the community and for the altar to take the form of a table around which the people of God could gather for the eucharistic feast.

1 Our Church Welcomes Us

O God, you have brought us here together.
We give you thanks and praise.

Based on Eucharistic Prayer for Masses with Children I

Share

A community is a place where people make you
feel welcome.

In a family community, people share life and love.

In a neighborhood, people live near each other.

In a classroom, people learn together.

What communities make you feel welcome?

_____

----

1. I belong to the _____ family.

   _____

   ----

2. I live on _____ Street.

How is the Catholic Church a community?

A Warm Welcome

One day, Jesus met a man who collected taxes. His name was Levi. Jesus asked, "Levi, will you follow me?"

"Of course I will," Levi answered. He was happy to become a follower of Jesus.

That night, Levi invited Jesus and his friends to his home. Jesus was the guest of honor. Levi made Jesus and his friends feel very welcome!

Based on Luke 5:27–29

God's People

Levi invited Jesus and his friends to dinner. Levi made his guests feel very welcome. Our Church invites us to celebrate a special meal, too. Our church community welcomes us. The special meal we celebrate is the Mass. It celebrates God's love for us. We are God's People.

Our Church Teaches

We call the Church the **Body of Christ**. A body has many parts. There are eyes, ears, arms, legs, hands, and feet. The body needs all its parts. The Church needs all its people. The Church is the Body of Christ.

We Believe

We are God's People. We are the Body of Christ.

Faith Words

Body of Christ
The Catholic Church is the Body of Christ.

How do church members act?

Respond

Welcome, Neighbors!

Tommy and his family came to the United States to escape a war in their country. Soldiers had put them out of their home.

Father Louis and the people of St. John's parish decided to help. Father Louis let the family live in a house owned by the Church. Some families brought food and clothes. Others brought books and toys. A teacher in the parish is teaching Tommy's family to speak English. Father Louis helped Tommy's dad find a job.

? How do the people of St. John's parish show that they are God's People?

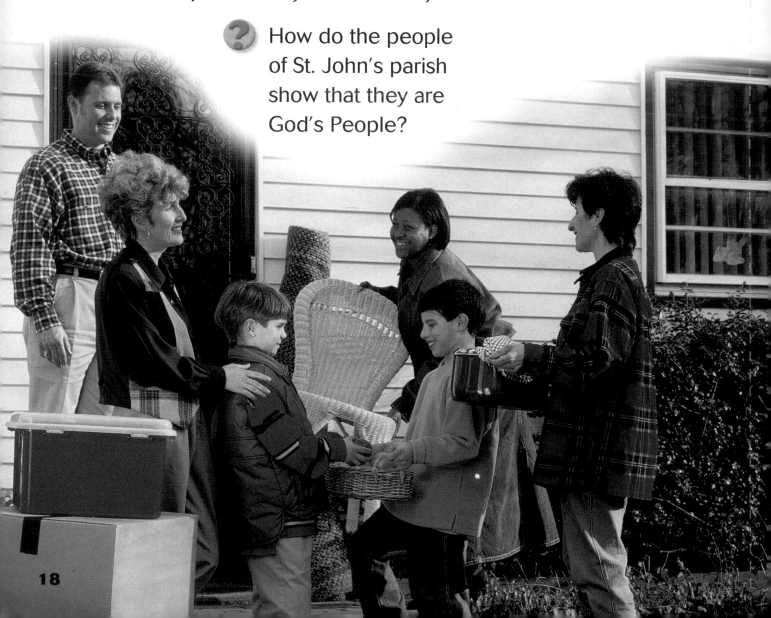

Activities

1. In the box, draw a picture of people who are caring for others.

2. Talk about ways to make other people feel welcome.

How can we celebrate being God's People?

Prayer Celebration

We Are God's People

We celebrate being God's People by praying together.

We welcome others by holding hands.

Leader: Sing with joy to God!
Be glad to serve the Lord.

All: We are God's People.

Leader: God made us.
He calls us together as one Church.

All: We are God's People.

Leader: Give thanks to God,
who is always good.
Be joyful, for his kindness lasts forever.

All: We are God's People,
the Body of Christ.

Based on Psalm 100

FAMILY TIME

A choice of things to do at home

We Belong to the Church

This chapter is a description of the journey your child has begun in the faith. Baptism, Confirmation, and Eucharist initiate us into the Body of Christ. These sacraments use common elements, such as water, bread, and oil, as signs of our membership in the Church.

Water, water, everywhere!

Serve glasses of water with dinner tonight. Ask questions, such as *How does it taste? What foods on the table were made with water? How did each of us use water today?*

Alone or with a group

Together, discuss activities that are done alone and those done with a group. Make a chart with two columns and the headings *Alone* and *With a Group*. Write each activity under its heading. Prompt your child to include some church-related activities.

Signs of Baptism

Show pictures of Baptisms of family members. Discuss the signs of white clothes, blessed water, oil, and a lighted candle.

✝ A Prayer for the Week

We thank you, God, for giving us life. Help us live each day as your chosen ones. Help us treat each other with love. Amen.

FAMILY TIME

Something to Do . . .

On Sunday

Upon entering church, use the holy water font and make the Sign of the Cross. Remember your membership in the Church as a follower of Jesus.

Through the Week

Discuss ways to show others your belief in God's unconditional love, such as community volunteer work.

Visit Our Web Site

 www.blestarewe.com

Something to Know About . . .

Our Heritage in Art

The Baptism of Christ by Piero della Francesca is one of the finest paintings of the Italian Renaissance. The painting is now in the National Gallery in London, but it was originally an altarpiece in the chapel of St. John the Baptist in Piero's native town, Sansepolcro, in central Italy.

The painting illustrates the exact moment of Christ's baptism when Saint John pours water from a bowl over Christ as the Holy Spirit descends from heaven.

Something to Think About . . .

A Community of Faith

I baptize you in the name of the Father, and of the Son, and of the Holy Spirit.
Rite of Baptism for Children

Jesus gathered others around him to form a community. As time went on, they realized who Jesus was and what they were called to do as his followers. As others joined these original disciples, the Church was formed. Each new member was initiated into this community of faith.

Our membership in the Church is both an honor and a responsibility. We have been given faith by God so that others will come to see in us the reflection of God's unconditional love for all. Our model is Jesus, who is the very Word of God made flesh. In all his words and actions, Jesus was a sign of God's love.

2 We Belong to the Church

We are children of the light.
We are children of the day.

Based on 1 Thessalonians 5:5

Share

People have many ways to show they belong to a certain group.

Look at these pictures.
Match each sign of belonging with its group.
Then tell about a sign of belonging that you have.

SIGN   **GROUP**

What signs of belonging do church members have?

23

The Sacraments

There are three sacraments of belonging. In **Baptism** we become new members of the Church. In **Confirmation** we receive strength to follow Jesus. In **Eucharist** we share a special meal with Jesus.

The Church uses many signs to celebrate Baptism.

1. The priest or deacon pours blessed water over the child or places the child in water. At the same time he says, "I baptize you in the name of the Father, and of the Son, and of the Holy Spirit."

2. The priest or deacon makes the Sign of the Cross on the child's forehead. He does this with blessed oil.

3. Next, the child receives white clothes. The priest or deacon says, "You have become new. You have put on Christ."

4. **Then the child's godparents receive a lighted candle. The priest or deacon says, "Receive the light of Christ."**

Signs of God's Love

A **sacrament** is a special celebration of the Church. The sacraments are signs that God is here with us now.

The three **sacraments of belonging, or initiation**, celebrate our new life with Jesus in the Church.

Our Church Teaches

Soon after God created people, they sinned by disobeying God. This first sin is called **original sin**. Because we are born with original sin, it is harder for us to do what is right. Baptism takes away original sin and all other sin. We are filled with the Holy Spirit. We are the children of God.

Respond
Bringing Light to Others

"What a great day!" thought Rita. "The new twins in our family, Samuel and Joshua, were baptized today. Someday, I will tell them all about the ceremony. I'll tell them about the beautiful Easter candle. It reminds us that Jesus is the Light of the World.

"I will tell them that their godfather, Uncle Al, lit two small candles from the Easter candle. The small candles remind us to keep the light of Jesus alive inside us. They remind us to bring Christ's light to others by our words and actions.

"Sam and Josh are already bringing light into my life!"

? What are some ways you can bring God's light to others?

Activity

Use these words to complete the puzzle.

> belonging   **Light**   sacrament
> children   **Water**

Down

1. Baptism is a sign of ____ to the Church.

3. ____ is used in Baptism.

Across

2. We are ____ of God.

4. A ____ is a sign of God's love.

5. The Easter candle reminds us that Jesus is the ____ of the World.

How can we celebrate that we are God's children?

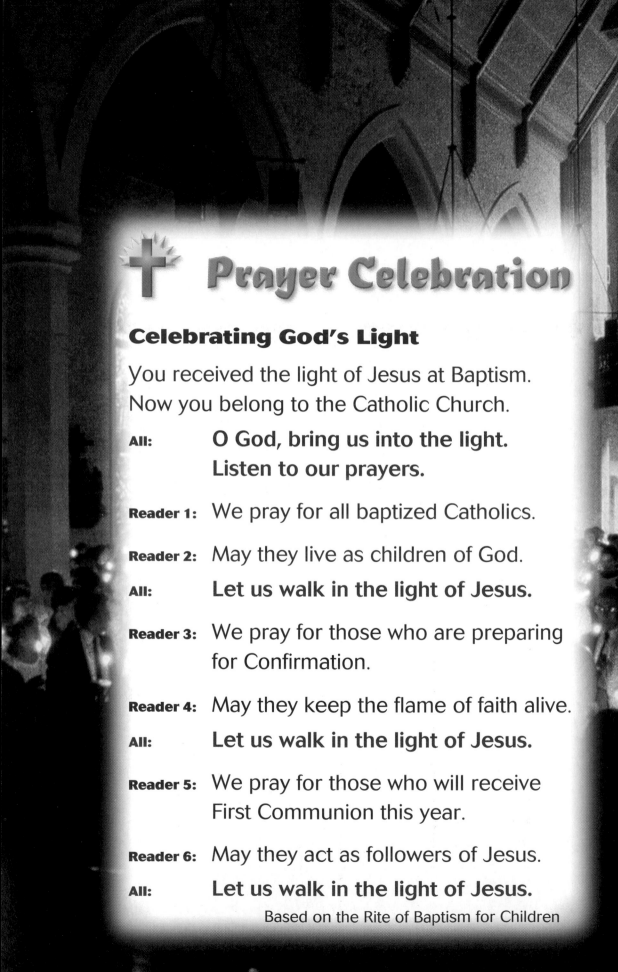

✝ Prayer Celebration

Celebrating God's Light

You received the light of Jesus at Baptism.
Now you belong to the Catholic Church.

All: **O God, bring us into the light.
Listen to our prayers.**

Reader 1: We pray for all baptized Catholics.

Reader 2: May they live as children of God.

All: **Let us walk in the light of Jesus.**

Reader 3: We pray for those who are preparing
for Confirmation.

Reader 4: May they keep the flame of faith alive.

All: **Let us walk in the light of Jesus.**

Reader 5: We pray for those who will receive
First Communion this year.

Reader 6: May they act as followers of Jesus.

All: **Let us walk in the light of Jesus.**

Based on the Rite of Baptism for Children

FAMILY TIME

A choice of things to do at home

Our Church Shows Us How to Live

Jesus shows us how to live in a way that pleases God. The saints have also shown us different ways to live a life that is godlike. The saints were men and women of various social and economic circumstances who lived extraordinary lives. They had this in common: They tried to live by the commandments, to love God, and to love their neighbors.

Name the saints

Together, pick out an admirable quality or virtue possessed by each family member, and then have a "saint-making" ceremony. Someone might be the saint of car repairs, and someone else might be the saint of kindness. Make a badge for each family saint with the person's name and "saintly" quality. Then present the badges at your ceremony.

Find your saint

Are some family members named after saints? With your child, learn about these saints. Find out when their feast days are celebrated.

Make a shrine

You and your child can make a small shrine to honor a favorite saint. Draw a picture of the saint you want to honor and paste it on cardboard. Paste decorations around the picture. Display the shrine in your home. You and your child can say a prayer to your saint in front of the shrine.

A Prayer for the Week

We thank you, God, for giving us Jesus, Mary, and the saints to show us how to live. Please give us the strength to live like them. Amen.

FAMILY TIME

Something to Do . . .

On Sunday

Are there statues of saints in your church? Are any saints pictured in the stained-glass windows? Whose images do you see?

Through the Week

Listen for references to the names of saints, such as St. Louis (the city) and the New Orleans Saints football team.

Visit Our Web Site

 www.blestarewe.com

Something to Think About . . .

The Good Samaritan

But a Samaritan traveler who came upon him was moved with compassion at the sight.
Luke 10:33

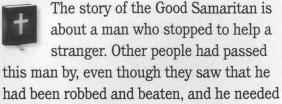

The story of the Good Samaritan is about a man who stopped to help a stranger. Other people had passed this man by, even though they saw that he had been robbed and beaten, and he needed help badly. The man who stopped took care of the stranger's wounds and took him to an inn. Then the man gave the innkeeper money to continue caring for the injured man.

The Samaritan acted in the way that Jesus expects us to act. Jesus asks us to be good neighbors. It is not always convenient to stop to help someone, but that is what Jesus calls us to do.

Something to Know About . . . Our Heritage in Literature

The story of the Good Samaritan is famous. Many people know about the kind man who stopped to help the hurt stranger. The story is so famous that a good samaritan law has been enacted. This law requires people who have medical training to stop and help when they see an accident.

There was a time when those who had medical training wouldn't stop because they were afraid of being sued. This law protects the "Good Samaritans" from being sued, while requiring them to use their training to help the injured.

3 Our Church Shows Us How to Live

 Love one another. Then everyone will know that you are my followers.

Based on John 13:35

Share

Some people are heroes. They help others.
They show us how to live.

Find the heroes in these pictures.
Draw circles around them.

Who is your favorite real-life hero? Why?

Who are the Church's heroes?

✝ The Real Hero

One day, Jesus told a story about a hero.

A man was traveling by himself. Robbers attacked him. They beat him and took his money. He was left lying in the road, badly hurt.

Soon a priest came by. He saw the man, but he just kept going.

Next, a man who worked in the Temple came along. He also passed by without helping.

Then, a third man came by, riding a donkey. He was from the country of Samaria. When he saw the hurt man on the road, he stopped at once. He washed the man's wounds and bandaged them. Then the man from Samaria put the hurt man on the donkey. He took him to an inn. There he paid the innkeeper to care for the man.

Based on Luke 10:29-35

Heroes of Our Church

The Church has many heroes who are like the good man from Samaria. The Church has Mary, the mother of Jesus, and the **saints**. From these church heroes we learn how to be **holy**. We learn how to be good followers of Jesus.

Our Church Teaches

All people are made to be like God. Through Baptism we are called to live good and holy lives. We become good and holy by following the example of Jesus, Mary, and the saints.

We Believe

We grow in holiness by living in love. We grow in love for God and others through constant practice.

Faith Words

saint

A saint is a person who shows great love for other people and for God.

holy

To be holy means to be like God. Holy people act like Jesus.

How can we imitate Mary and the saints?

Respond

Mary and the Saints

Mary and the saints teach us how to live as Christians.

Mary is the greatest saint of all. She was a good mother to Jesus. She teaches us to trust God and to care for others.

Saint Peter Claver cared for people nobody else cared about. He teaches us to reach out in love to everyone in need.

Saint Brigid sold her belongings and gave the money to poor people. She teaches us to share our blessings with others.

Saint Jerome loved to teach people how to read and understand the Bible. He teaches us to share the word of God with others.

The Church has many heroes like this.
They all teach us how to love God and follow Jesus.

 Which saint is your favorite?
How can you follow this saint's example?

Activity

Draw a picture of someone you know who is a hero. Or draw a picture that shows <u>you</u> acting as a real-life hero.

How can we ask holy people to pray for us?

Prayer Celebration

Litany of Saints and Heroes

A litany is a prayer that is said aloud.
A leader names different saints or other
holy people.
After each name we ask the saint or person
to pray for us.

Leader:	All:
Holy Mary, Mother of God,	pray for us.
Saint Peter Claver,	pray for us.
Saint Brigid,	pray for us.
Saint Jerome,	pray for us.
All who help the poor and the hungry,	pray for us.
All who care for the weak and the sick,	pray for us.
All holy men and women,	pray for us.

All: **Heavenly God, may we follow the example of your saints and other holy people. May we always try to help people in need. Amen.**

FAMILY TIME

A choice of things to do at home

We Praise and Thank God

Saint Augustine said those who sing pray twice. He was telling us that raising our voices in song pleases God. This chapter presents the value of song as a form of prayer and the value of prayers of thanks and praise.

Praise always

Help your child to praise each person in your family this week. Assist your child by helping to write a list of family members, with praises for each one. The list will help your child say something complimentary to each family member.

Sing grace

Sing a grace before meals if you know one. One example is "Evening has come, the board is spread. Thanks be to God, who gives us bread." Explain that *board* is another word for "table" and that the board is *spread,* or covered, with food and beverages.

Name that hymn

Play "Name That Hymn!" with your family. You can hum, play a musical instrument, or sing "la-la-la" to the tune of a favorite hymn. Let the others guess the title. Then invite them to sing along, if they know the words.

✝ **A Prayer for the Week**

Thank you, Lord, for giving us life. Thank you for giving us each other. And thank you for giving us everlasting life.
Amen.

FAMILY TIME

Something to Do . . .

On Sunday

Even if you don't usually join in the singing at Mass, try it this week. Then, as Saint Augustine said, you will "pray twice."

Through the Week

Each day think of something you are grateful for. It might be a sunset, a cup of cocoa, or a talk with a friend.

Visit Our Web Site

 www.blestarewe.com

Something to Think About . . .

Giving Thanks and Praise

It is good to give thanks to the LORD, to sing praise to your name, Most High.
Psalm 92:2

Some people look on the gloomy side of life. They don't see what there is to be happy about. They don't understand that all creation is a gift from God. We don't earn all the wonderful things we have in this life. They are gifts to us, and our only job is to be thankful for receiving them.

This chapter includes the story of King David, a musician who praised God and gave him thanks through joyful song. When we go to Mass, we praise God and give him thanks as we sing the Gloria together. In this chapter your child will learn part of the Gloria.

Something to Know About . . . Our Heritage in Music

Since the seventh century the Church has been expressing its praise of God musically through Gregorian chant. Named after Pope Gregory I, chant is a solemn form of singing that creates a harmony between words and melody. Because in some pagan religions music was used to stir up people, Christians were encouraged to have a kind of music that was prayerful. Gregorian chant met that standard. There were other kinds of chants before Gregorian chant, but it was more beautiful and developed than some of the others.

In recent years a group of monks put out a recording called *Chant* that proved to be very popular. It revived interest in Gregorian chant.

4 We Praise and Thank God

Sing to the LORD a new song.

Psalm 149:1

Share

Celebrations are important times.
People come together to give thanks.
They say "thank you" for special people or gifts.

 On the Fourth of July, we give thanks for freedom.

 On birthdays we give thanks for life.

 On Thanksgiving we give thanks for all our blessings.

 On Valentine's Day we give thanks for friends.

1. Write the name of a celebration you enjoyed.

Thanksgiveing Christmis

2. Write why you gave thanks.

becuase I like to celebrat jeusess birthday.

Why do God's People give thanks?

Hear & Believe

King David Gives Thanks

King David loved God. He liked to lead people in prayer. David especially liked to play the harp and sing. He sang about God's goodness. He thanked God for giving the people many gifts.

One day the priests carried into David's city the ark that held God's laws. David greeted the ark with joyful dancing. He ordered the musicians to play on their harps, lyres, and cymbals. Then David sang out,

"How good it is to give God thanks and glory!
I sing praise to your name, Most High.
Every morning you are kind to me.
You are with me all day and all night.
Your goodness fills me with gladness.
I rejoice because of the gifts you give me."

Based on 1 Chronicles 15 and Psalm 92:1–5

40

We Give Praise and Thanks

At Mass our parish community celebrates in prayer and in song. We **praise** God for his goodness. We also give God thanks.

Our Church Teaches

Prayer is talking to and listening to God. There are different types of prayer. Some prayers praise God. Some prayers give him thanks. We can pray silently or out loud. We can pray alone or with others. We can pray with words and with holy music.

How can we praise and thank God?

Respond
Glory to God

In the first part of the Mass, we usually sing "Glory to God." This special song is called the Gloria. It is a prayer of praise and thanks. This is how it begins.

> Glory to God in the highest,
> and peace to his people on earth.
>
> Lord God, heavenly King,
> almighty God and Father,
> we worship you, we give you thanks,
> we praise you for your glory.

The Order of Mass

Activities

1. Write your own prayer of thanks.

   O God, I thank you for

   _____

   -

   _____

   -

   _____

   -

   _____

2. Write your own prayer of praise.

   O God, I praise you for being

   _____

   -

   _____

   -

   _____

   -

   _____

You will use these prayers in
the Prayer Celebration.

**How can we
praise and
thank God
with song?**

43

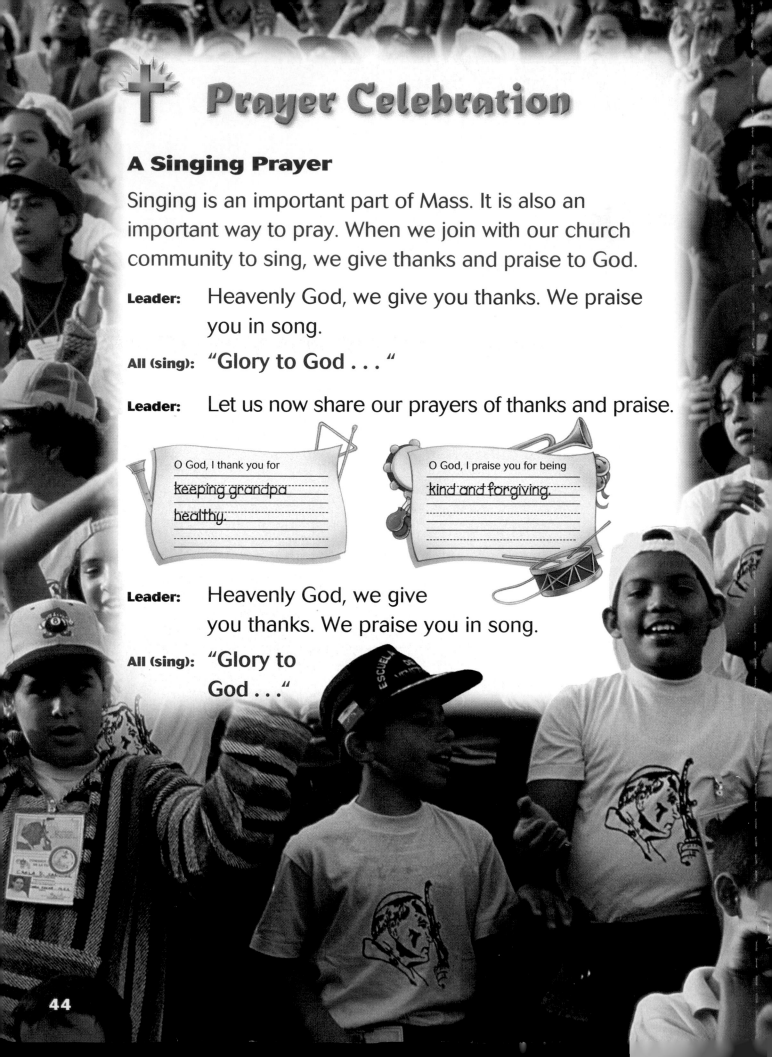

✝ Prayer Celebration

A Singing Prayer

Singing is an important part of Mass. It is also an important way to pray. When we join with our church community to sing, we give thanks and praise to God.

Leader: Heavenly God, we give you thanks. We praise you in song.

All (sing): "Glory to God . . . "

Leader: Let us now share our prayers of thanks and praise.

O God, I thank you for
keeping grandpa
healthy.

O God, I praise you for being
kind and forgiving.

Leader: Heavenly God, we give you thanks. We praise you in song.

All (sing): "Glory to God . . ."

The Gift

Zack thought, "My godmother's birthday is coming. I want to buy her a present, but I don't have any money."

Then Zack remembered what he learned in art class. He could make a pretty picture frame! So he asked his Mom for a photograph from the family album.

Then Zack drew a picture. It showed him with his godmother on the day he was baptized. Then he glued colored toothpicks into the shapes of four candles, one for each corner of the picture frame.

When Zack gave the picture to his godmother, he was proud. He said, "This gift did not cost any money. I made it for you myself."

"Great!" said Zack's godmother. "Money couldn't buy anything as wonderful as this. Thanks, Zack."

Sometimes the best gifts don't cost money. Why?

Think About It

Zack used something he had learned to make a gift. Read about learning and sharing below. Color the box blue if you agree. If you do not agree, color the box red.

Learning new things

☐ always costs money

☐ challenges you to make discoveries

Sharing what you learned

☐ is not a good idea

☐ helps others to grow

Learn About It

Saints are good and holy people. They use the things they have learned to help others. We follow their example when we share the things we learn.

Do Something About It

Maybe you have learned to do something special. Or you could start to learn something now.

Use a ✔ to show things you can already do.

☐ give someone a big smile

☐ teach someone to play a game

☐ make a gift for someone

Use a ✔ to show things you want to learn to do.

☐ teach a pet to do tricks

☐ take photographs

☐ play a musical instrument

Use the words below to complete the sentences.

welcomes	thank	live	belong

1 Our Church _____ us.

2 We _____ to the Church.

3 Our Church shows us how to _____ _____.

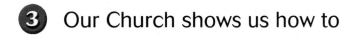

4 We praise and _____ _____ God.

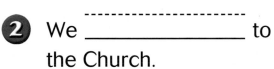

Review

A Circle the correct answer.

1. Catholics are ____ People.
   America's   God's

2. The Church is the Body of ____.
   Christ   John

3. The body needs all its parts, and the Church needs all its ____.
   pews   people

4. Our Church invites us to celebrate a special ____.
   meal   parade

5. The special meal is called the ____.
   Mass   Mission

B Draw a line from the name of each sacrament of initiation to its meaning.

1. Baptism   •   • to share a special meal with Jesus

2. Confirmation •   • to become a member of the Church

3. Eucharist   •   • to receive strength to follow Jesus

C Remember the story about the good man from Samaria. Then put the story in order. Write the numbers 1, 2, and 3 in the boxes.

☐ The man from Samaria helped the man who was hurt.

☐ Robbers beat a traveler and hurt him badly.

☐ Two men passed by without helping the hurt man.

D Use the words below to complete the sentences.

Mary   love   God   saint   holy

_____
----

1. A _____ is a person who shows great

_____

_____ for other people and for God.

_____
----

2. To be _____ means to be

_____
----

like _____.

_____
----

3. _____ and the saints teach us how to live as Christians.

Review

E Remember the story "King David Gives Thanks."
Then draw a line under each set of words that
names something King David liked to do.

mop the floor   lead people in prayer

sing and dance   run in races

get a haircut   give thanks to God

F Use a ✔ to mark the sentences that are true.

☐ **1.** Prayer is talking to and listening to God.

☐ **2.** Praise is a sad kind of prayer.

☐ **3.** We usually sing the Gloria at Mass.

☐ **4.** There is only one kind of prayer.

☐ **5.** We pray when we sing holy songs.

We Ask God's Forgiveness

God is always ready to forgive us when we sin. God calls us to be sorry for the wrongs we have done. He wants us to forgive others who have wronged us.

Rejoice with me because I have found my lost sheep.

Luke 15:6

God is like a shepherd who is happy to find his lost sheep. God rejoices when we are sorry for our sins.

Psalm 51: Be Merciful, O Lord

Psalm 51

Music by Marty Haugen

VERSE

1. Have mercy on me, God, in your kindness,
   in your compassion, blot out my offense.
   O wash me more and more from my guilt and my sorrow,
   and cleanse me from all of my sin.
   Refrain

2. My offenses, truly I know them,
   and my sins are always before me;
   against you alone have I sinned, O Lord,
   what is evil in your sight I have done.
   Refrain

3. Create in me a clean heart, O God,
   put your steadfast spirit in my soul.
   Cast me not away from your presence, O Lord,
   and take not your spirit from me.
   Refrain

4. Give back to me the joy of your salvation,
   let your willing spirit bear me up
   and I shall teach your way to the ones who have wandered,
   and bring them all home to your side.
   Refrain

FAMILY TIME

A choice of things to do at home

We Can Choose What Is Good

Saint Thomas Aquinas, a Dominican priest and great theologian, proclaimed that humans always tended toward the good. But how do we figure out what the good is? It may feel good to finish the last of a box of candy, but others in our family might not see it as good. We try to form a good conscience to help us identify what is good and then try to conform our behavior to our conscience. Being Catholic helps us understand that God gives us free choice, and yet he is always ready to forgive us when we choose to sin.

I'm sorry

Explain to your child that one of the choices we have if we do something hurtful is to say "I'm sorry." Encourage your child to write a card, send an e-mail, or make a phone call if an apology needs to be made.

Good choice

Together, talk about something your child did recently that was good and something else that was not good. Ask why one thing was good and the other was not. Then remind your child that a person can always choose to do good.

Pick-up sticks

Have you ever played pick-up sticks? If you have, you know that the sticks fall and you have to pick them up without moving any stick except the one you are removing. Play pick-up sticks with your child. Think about how the game is like making moral choices. You need to choose carefully in order to succeed.

✚ A Prayer for the Week

Lord, thank you for the gift of free choice. Help us use this gift to make right choices and remain free of sin. Amen.

FAMILY TIME

Something to Do . . .

On Sunday

During the Penitential Rite, reflect on the choices you made during the week. Thank God for his guidance.

Through the Week

As a family, watch one TV show. Discuss the choices the characters made. Which were good? Which were bad?

Visit Our Web Site

 www.blestarewe.com

Something to Know About . . .

Our Heritage in Art

The Rembrandt painting titled *Return of the Prodigal Son* depicts the story Jesus told of the young man who left his family and squandered his fortune. Thinking he would be better off as a servant on his father's farm than living as he was—poor, hungry, and alone—he returned home. As this painting shows, his father welcomed him back as a son, not as a servant.

Something to Think About . . .

A Warm Welcome

I shall say to him, "Father, I have sinned against heaven and against you."
Luke 15:18

The story of the Prodigal Son tells about a man whose younger son took his inheritance, moved away from home, and wasted the money. When he was poor and hungry, the son returned home. He asked for his father's forgiveness and offered to work as a hired hand.

The father rejoiced when the son returned. He told his servants, "Quickly bring the finest robe and put it on him; put a ring on his finger and sandals on his feet. Take the fattened calf and slaughter it. Then let us celebrate with a feast, because this son of mine was dead, and has come to life again" (Luke 15:22–24).

Like the father in the Scripture, God, our Father, is always ready to forgive us.

5 We Can Choose What Is Good

 Love the LORD, your God, and obey his word.

Based on Deuteronomy 30:20

Share

We make many choices every day. Some choices are easy, but some are hard. Some are right, but others are wrong.

Draw a happy face for each good choice below. Draw a sad face for each bad choice.

1. Tom does not share with his friends.

2. Juanita tells her dad the truth.

3. Wes obeys his mom and turns off the TV.

4. Mary takes a dollar that is not hers.

How do we know what is right and wrong?

✝ The Forgiving Father

Once there was a man who had two sons. The younger son said, "I know you plan to give me money when I am older. May I have it now?" So his father gave him the money.

The boy moved far away. In no time at all, he had spent every cent! He was hungry and had no place to live. He wanted to go home.

The boy was sorry for the wrong choices he had made. He had wasted the money and hurt his father. The boy decided to ask his father to take him back.

While the boy was still far off from home, his father saw him and ran to greet him. "I'm sorry," the boy said, but his father had already forgiven him. The man hugged his son and gave him new clothes. Then he gave the boy a big "welcome home" party.

Based on Luke 15:11–24

Knowing Right from Wrong

The boy in the story knew he had done wrong. His **conscience** told him so. God gave everybody a conscience. Our conscience tells us the difference between what is right and wrong.

Our Church Teaches

We **sin** when we freely choose to do bad things. When we sin, we hurt our friendship with God and with other people. God wants us to be sorry for our sins. God loves us very much, and he is always ready to forgive us.

We Believe

God wants us to choose good and stay away from evil. But God lets us decide what to do. We call this **free choice.**

Faith Words

conscience
Our conscience helps us know right from wrong.

sin
We sin when we choose to hurt others and turn away from God.

How can we practice making good choices?

57

Respond

Making Good Choices

Mrs. Rabbit said, "Peter, you and your sisters may play outdoors. But stay away from Mr. McGregor's garden!"

Peter's sisters obeyed their mother, but Peter made a bad choice. He went into the garden and ate a lot of vegetables. Then Mr. McGregor saw Peter and began to chase him. Peter ran home as fast as he could.

Peter felt sick from eating so much. So Mrs. Rabbit gave him a hot drink and put him to bed. He missed having a nice supper with his mom and his sisters.

? What bad choice did Peter make?

Activity

We can practice making good choices every day. Unscramble the letters to complete the sentence for each picture.

t h g i f

Joey chooses not to

fight.

r h a s e

Tonya is happy to

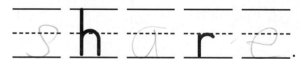
share.

t r t u h

Lily decides to tell the

truth.

How can we celebrate the gift of free choice?

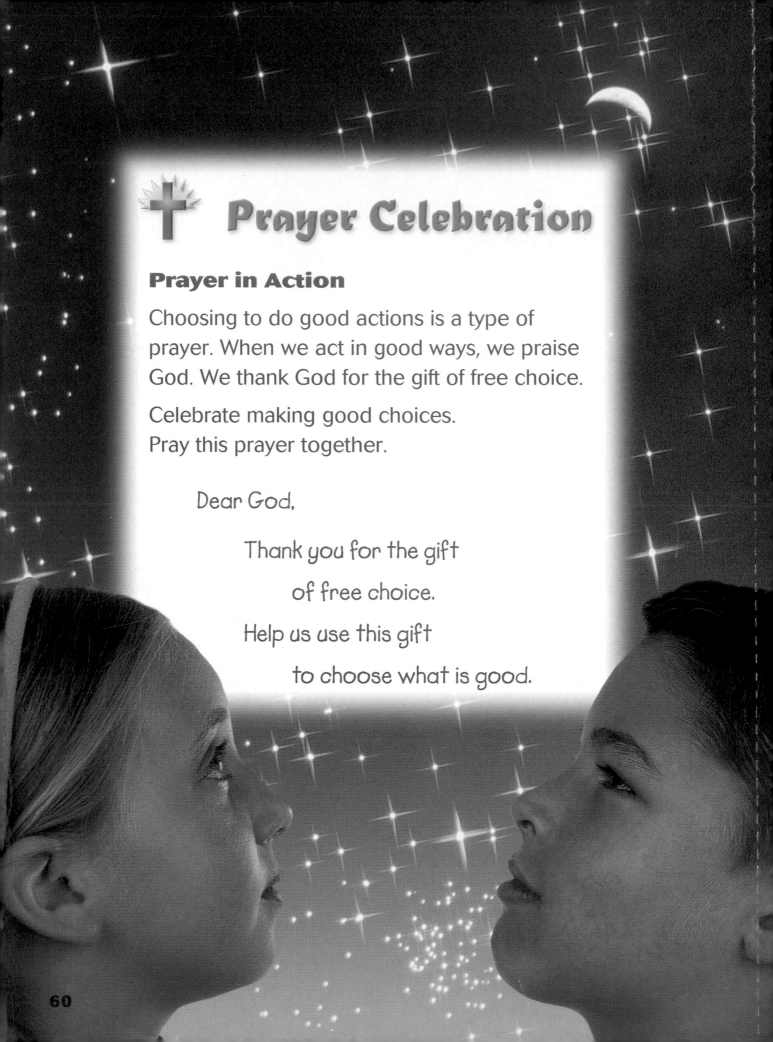

✝ Prayer Celebration

Prayer in Action

Choosing to do good actions is a type of prayer. When we act in good ways, we praise God. We thank God for the gift of free choice.

Celebrate making good choices.
Pray this prayer together.

Dear God,

Thank you for the gift

of free choice.

Help us use this gift

to choose what is good.

FAMILY TIME

A choice of things to do at home

We Celebrate God's Forgiveness

One of the great joys of Christian life is that we can always trust in God's mercy. When we ask for God's mercy and are forgiven, we are reconciled to God. Even though we turn away from God when we sin, God never turns away from us. He is always ready to welcome us back.

Edmund

In the book *The Lion, the Witch and the Wardrobe* by C. S. Lewis, Edmund betrays his brother and sisters and the lion, Aslan. Aslan forgives him. Rent the video of this fine book. Watch it together as a family.

Saying "I'm sorry"

Have you noticed differences in how family members ask for forgiveness? When you are together, in the car or at the table, talk about how the people in your family show that they are sorry or ask for forgiveness.

Pretzels

Buy some frozen bread dough and thaw it. With your child, break off pretzel-sized pieces and roll them into ropes. To make a pretzel shape, form a loop and then bring the ends of the loop up and cross them. Sprinkle salt on the pretzels and bake them. Point out to your child that the pretzel shape represents an attitude of prayer, with arms crossed.

✝ A Prayer for the Week

I'm sorry, Lord, for the things
I have done to hurt others. Help me
forgive others when they hurt me.
Merciful God, I trust in your
love and forgiveness.
Amen.

FAMILY TIME

Something to Do . . .

On Sunday

During the prayer before communion, "Lord, I am not worthy...," remember that God is always ready to forgive.

Through the Week

If anyone in your family does something wrong, be forgiving. You will act as a model for your child.

Visit Our Web Site

www.blestarewe.com

Something to Think About . . .

God's Healing Presence

May almighty God have mercy on us, forgive us our sins, and bring us to everlasting life.
The Order of Mass

We experience God's healing presence in the Penitential Rite of the Mass. It is a weekly time to review our behavior and accept responsibility for falling short of the demands that our Christianity makes on us. We are given a chance to start the new week with a clean slate.

Since younger children need role models, the adults and older children in your family should make a regular practice of attending parish Reconciliation services or celebrating private Reconciliation.

Something to Know About . . .

Our Heritage

Pope John Paul II apologized to the Jewish people for the prejudice some Catholics have shown them throughout history. He asked the Jews for forgiveness. This was an important decision. The Pope was speaking as the head of the Catholic Church, in the name of all its members. In speaking to all of the Jewish people, he apologized for all the injustices inflicted upon the Jews by any Catholic people. It was an important move toward reconciliation between two peoples who worship the same God.

6 We Celebrate God's Forgiveness

 Lord, you are kind and forgiving.

Based on Psalm 86:5

Share

Sometimes we say or do things that hurt other people. We can lose their friendship.

Put the pictures in order. In the boxes write 1, 2, 3, and 4 to tell a story about losing a friend and then making up.

How can we make up with God?

Hear & Believe

Making Up

The sacrament of **Reconciliation**, or Penance, celebrates the gift of God's forgiveness. Here is what happens in the sacrament.

Welcome Father Lee greets Pat in the reconciliation room. They read from the Bible. They hear how God loves us and is always ready to forgive us.

Confession Pat talks about, or **confesses**, her sins. Father Lee helps her find ways to do better. He asks her to say a prayer or do a kind act to make up for what she has done wrong. This prayer or action is called a **penance**.

Prayer of Sorrow Pat says a prayer of sorrow, called the Act of Contrition. She tells God she is sorry and will try not to sin again.

Absolution Father Lee prays for Pat and asks God to forgive her. He gives Pat **absolution** in the name of the Father, Son, and Holy Spirit. Absolution is the forgiveness of God, given through the priest in this sacrament. Then Father Lee gives thanks and says, "Go in peace." Pat answers, "Amen."

A Sacrament of Healing

When we have sinned, we need to say we are sorry. We need forgiveness. The sacrament of Reconciliation celebrates God's forgiveness. God invites us to be at peace again.

Our Church Teaches

The sacrament of Reconciliation helps us make peace with God and the Church.

The gift of God's **grace** helps us stay away from sin. Grace is God's loving presence in our lives.

How can we practice being people who forgive?

Respond
Time to Forgive

Andy and Mark's father built them a treehouse. It was the best treehouse in the neighborhood. Andy wanted to play in it with his friends. He did not want his little brother Mark around.

One day, Mark just couldn't wait any longer for his turn. So he climbed up the ladder. "It's my turn now," he said with a frown.

Andy pushed him away. Mark fell off the ladder and broke his leg. He had to wear a heavy cast for a long time. Andy felt sorry for what had happened. He had not meant to hurt Mark.

? How could Andy make up with Mark?

Activities

1. Complete the sentences with these forgiveness words.

sorry   forgive   make up

Andy and Mark should _that tirns_.

Andy should say to Mark, "I am _so, so, sorry_."

Mark should say to Andy, "I _forgive_ you."

2. Write 1, 2, 3, and 4 to put the parts of the sacrament of Reconciliation in order.

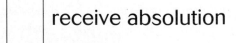

☐ pray a prayer of sorrow

☐ be given a penance

☐ receive absolution

☐ confess sins

How can we celebrate God's forgiveness?

Prayer Celebration

Lord, Have Mercy

During Mass, we tell God we are sorry for our sins. We ask God to have mercy on us. Mercy is a generous type of love. It leads to forgiveness.

Pray this prayer of reconciliation.

Leader: Lord Jesus, you help us live in peace with one another and with God the Father.

All: **Lord, have mercy.**

Leader: Lord Jesus, you heal the hurt that is caused by sin.

All: **Christ, have mercy.**

Leader: Lord Jesus, you pray to your Father for us.

All: **Lord, have mercy.**

Leader: May almighty God have mercy on us, forgive us our sins, and bring us to everlasting life.

All: **Amen.**

The Order of Mass

FAMILY TIME

A choice of things to do at home

We Think About Our Choices

This chapter deals with making choices and presents the Ten Commandments. The Commandments serve as a guide against which we measure our choices. Children learn that they are responsible for their actions. They learn that when they choose to do wrong, they sin. They also consider the differences among mistakes, venial sins, and mortal sins.

Watching a movie

Rent the movie *Searching for Bobby Fischer* and watch it with your family. It shows a boy with an unusual ability, and the decisions his parents make about his education. The parents work to help Bobby as well as they can, not always agreeing on what is the best way to help.

Following the rules

Discuss with your child rules around the house and at school. Talk about the purpose of rules. Ask what happens when the rules are not followed, and what happens when they are followed.

Choose a game

Play a board game as a family. Board games that involve choices help to illustrate the point of this chapter. Playing one of these games will demonstrate how the choices we make lead to consequences.

A Prayer for the Week

Thank you, Lord, for giving us the Ten Commandments. With your help, we believe that we can do better every day. Amen.

FAMILY TIME

Something to Do . . .

On Sunday

Talk with your family about ways to honor the Sabbath, such as going to Mass, avoiding conflict, and thinking about what God wants you to do.

Through the Week

Find examples of making everyday choices at home, work, and school. Which decisions are hardest to make?

Visit Our Web Site

 www.blestarewe.com

Something to Think About . . .

Making Choices

I, the LORD, am your God, who brought you out of the land of Egypt, that place of slavery.
Exodus 20:2

With these words God gave Moses the Ten Commandments. God was reminding Moses and the Israelites that he was there for them when they were in trouble. God wasn't going to ask his People to honor him and keep his commandments without reminding them that he was a loving, caring God.

When we make choices in our lives, we try to make them according to the commandments. It is good to remember that God is there to help us. God's faithfulness is an example for parents. We need to be there for our children, even though their behavior is not always as good as we might wish.

Something to Know About . . .

Our Heritage in Film

The movie *E.T.: The Extraterrestrial*, made in 1982 and directed by Steven Spielberg, is a story in which characters take care of an extraterrestrial that is lost on Earth. These children are forced to make a number of decisions, many of which involve concealing E.T. from adults. Right or wrong, the children make their choices to protect E.T. out of love. The most difficult decision the children make is to help E.T. return home, even though they will

miss the alien very much. E.T.'s relationship with Elliot, the main child character, is especially touching. The movie continues to be popular years after it was first shown.

7 We Think About Our Choices

Teach me, O LORD, your ways.
Guide me in goodness and truth.

Based on Psalm 25:4–5

Share

As we grow up, we learn to be responsible for our actions. We are responsible when we do our work. We are responsible when we take good care of things.

Check (✓) each sentence that tells about a responsibility you have.

☐ **1.** I feed the family pet.

☐ **2.** I help Mom and Dad.

☐ **3.** I do my homework.

☐ **4.** I listen to my teacher.

☐ **5.** I return my library books.

☐ **6.** I hang up my jacket.

Name some other responsibilities that you have.

How do church members show responsibility?

✝ Moses on the Mountain

Moses was on a mountaintop when God spoke to him. God wanted to help everyone lead good lives. He gave Moses the laws called the **Ten Commandments**. God called the Hebrew people to love him and respect him. The Ten Commandments reminded people to rest and pray on the Lord's day, to obey their parents, and to avoid telling lies or stealing. The Commandments also said not to hurt other people nor be jealous of them.

When God had finished, Moses went down the mountain. He told the people about these laws of God, the Ten Commandments.

Based on Exodus 20:1–17

The Ten Commandments

God gave us the Ten Commandments as special responsibilities. The Ten Commandments are God's laws. They help us know right from wrong. They help us think about and make good choices.

Our Church Teaches

When we know that something is wrong, and we do it anyway, we sin. Sin turns us away from God and other people. **Mortal sins** are serious sins that separate us from our friendship with God. **Venial sins** are less serious sins. They weaken our friendship with God, but do not take it away.

Faith Words

mortal sin
A mortal sin is a serious sin that separates us from our friendship with God.

venial sin
A venial sin is a less serious sin. It weakens our friendship with God.

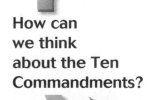

How can we think about the Ten Commandments?

73

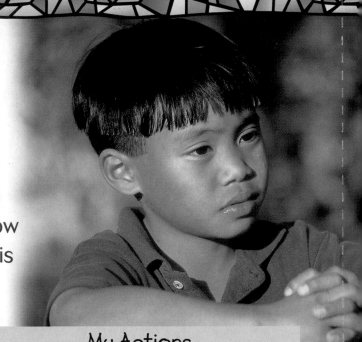

Respond

An Examination of Conscience

Before we celebrate the sacrament of Reconciliation, we think about the Ten Commandments. We ask ourselves how well we have followed each one. This is called an examination of conscience.

God's Laws	My Actions
1. Believe that there is only one God.	Do I believe in God and love God with all my heart?
2. Respect the name of God.	Do I use the names of God, Jesus, Mary, and the saints with respect?
3. Go to Mass on Sunday.	Do I celebrate Mass every Sunday?
4. Respect your father and mother.	Do I respect and obey my parents?
5. Take care of all that God has made.	Do I treat all God's creatures, especially people, with respect?
6. Treat your body as a gift from God.	Do I take good care of my body and respect the bodies of others?
7. Respect the property of others.	Have I taken something that belongs to someone else?
8. Always tell the truth.	Do I sometimes lie?
9. Respect the families of others.	Do I treat other families with respect?
10. Be content with what you have.	Am I ever jealous or greedy?

Mistakes and sins are not the same. You might break a glass by mistake. You sin when you choose to do something you know is wrong.

Activity

Follow the stone path. If a **mistake** is described on a stone, color the stone blue. If a **sin** is described, color the stone red.

1. Oops! I spilled gravy on my new sweater.

2. I stole my brother's favorite cap.

3. I had a big fight with a friend.

5. I was jealous of my friend's new bike.

4. I left the window open, and the rain came in.

6. I lied about what happened to my homework.

7. I lost my lunch money.

8. I forgot to wish my cousin a happy birthday.

How can we celebrate thinking about our choices?

← it's blue

Prayer Celebration

A Thinking Prayer

Thinking is a special gift God has given us. We can use this gift to think about our choices. We can also use it in prayer to ask God to forgive our sins.

Pray this thinking prayer together.

Leader: God, our Father, sometimes we have not behaved.

All: **But you love us and come to us.**

Leader: Sometimes we have caused trouble.

All: **But you love us and come to us.**

Leader: Sometimes we have argued.

All: **But you love us and come to us.**

Leader: Sometimes we have been lazy.

All: **But you love us and come to us.**

Leader: Sometimes we have told lies.

All: **But you love us and come to us.**

Based on the Rite of Penance

FAMILY TIME

A choice of things to do at home

We Say We Are Sorry

When we choose to do wrong, we need to say we are sorry, to God and to any person we have hurt. The focus of this chapter is to learn to use prayer to tell God that we are sorry. When we do this, we admit that we have done wrong and recognize that we need to acknowledge it. Children will learn that prayer brings us closer to God and that, with the Holy Spirit's help, we can change.

How many ways?

With your child, think of several ways to say or show that you are sorry. Some examples are "Please forgive me," "I didn't mean to hurt you," giving a hug, and shaking hands. You might want to make a list of all the expressions and actions you identified.

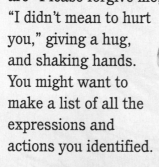

Sorry role-play

As a family, role-play situations from stories or TV episodes in which characters do something wrong and make an apology. For example, Cinderella's stepsisters have good reason to apologize!

Sorry state

"That's a sorry state you're in!" is an expression that means that something has gotten you into a mess. Talk about times when members of your family were in a "sorry state," needing to apologize to someone.

✝ A Prayer for the Week

Lord, as we look back on our day, we see some things to be sorry for. Please forgive us for our faults and help us do better. Amen.

FAMILY TIME

Something to Do . . .

On Sunday

During the Sunday liturgy, ask God's forgiveness for things that went wrong this week.

Through the Week

When stress occurs, call upon the Holy Spirit. Ask for God's grace to help you deal with your frustrations.

Visit Our Web Site

 www.blestarewe.com

Something to Think About . . .

The Power of Baptism

At that time Jerusalem, all Judea, and the whole region around the Jordan were going out to him and were being baptized by him in the Jordan River as they acknowledged their sins.

Matthew 3:5–6

Baptism brings forgiveness of all sins. The Church teaches that water is the symbol for cleansing away the stain of sin. Daily we recognize that water refreshes, renews, and gives new life. Baptized persons have the sinful state of humanity blessed in baptism. Even though we often make wrong choices, the power of baptism, which has made us followers of Christ, offers us God's forgiveness. We know that God will have mercy on us.

Something to Know About . . .

Our Heritage in Music

Fiddler on the Roof was a long-running Broadway musical and a successful movie. It tells the story of a Russian Jewish family before the Russian Revolution. One of the most poignant songs, "Sunrise, Sunset," sung by the mother and father, is about how quickly time passes in a family and how quickly children grow up. This song echoes the sentiment of most parents. How do children grow up so fast? This timely song reminds us that we should nurture our relationship with our children, because they won't be with us forever.

8 We Say We Are Sorry

When a sinner is sorry, there is great joy in heaven.

Based on Luke 15:7

Share

There are many ways to say "I'm sorry."
You can say it with words like "Let's make up."
You can say it with an action like a hug.
Tell another good way to say "I'm sorry."

Make a card to tell someone you are sorry for something. Print what you want to say.

Dear _____,

_____

_____

_____

_____

_____

Love,

_____

How can we tell God we are sorry?

Hear & Believe

✝ Return to God!

John the Baptizer was a very holy man. He told other people how to find God's forgiveness.

John: Return to God! Repent, for God's kingdom is coming!

Woman: What does repent mean?

John: Repent means to be truly sorry for your sins.

Boy: What else does repent mean?

John: It means that you really want to change.

Girl: Is that all we need to do to return to God?

John: No. You must also do **penance**. Penance is a prayer or an act to make up for the harm caused by sin.

Many people heard John's words. They confessed their sins. They told God they were sorry. Then John baptized them in the river.

Based on Matthew 3:1–8

Returning to God

Sin separates us from God. John the Baptizer wanted people to go back to God. We can return to God by telling him we are sorry for our sins. When we are sorry for our sins, we feel **contrition**. Contrition means to be sorry and to want to do better. To show that we are sorry, we pray an **act of contrition**. This is a prayer of sorrow. In this prayer we promise to try not to sin again.

Our Church Teaches

When we are truly sorry for our sins, the Holy Spirit helps us do better.

How can we show we are sorry for sin?

Respond

A Penance Service

Matt and Susan went to a penance service. Many other people were there, too. Everyone had come to show that they wanted to return to God. They listened to a story that Jesus once told about a shepherd and a lost sheep.

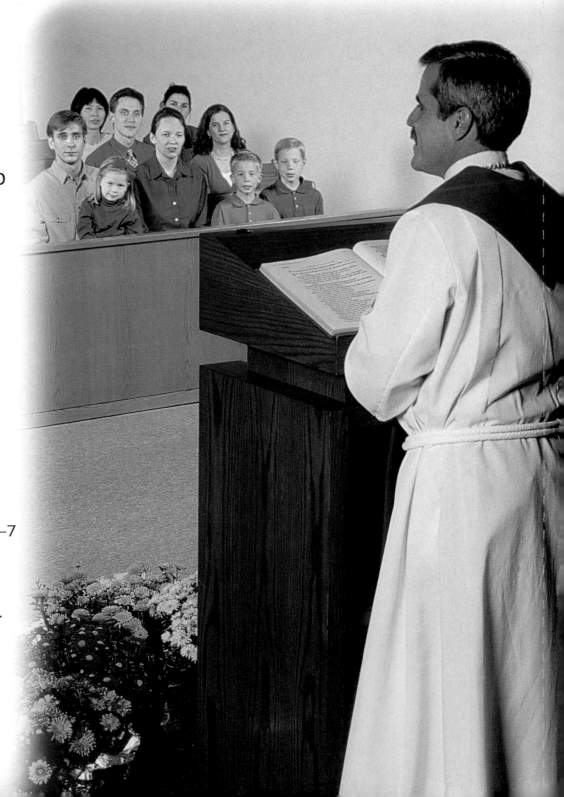

God is like the shepherd who had one hundred sheep. One sheep was lost, and the shepherd went to look for it. When he found the sheep, the shepherd was very happy. In the same way, there is great joy in heaven when a sinner is sorry.

Based on Luke 15:4–7

? Why is this a good story for a penance service?

Activity

Use the secret code to write the missing letters.

Then read the prayer of sorrow.

Secret Code

1	2	3	4	5	6	7	8	9	10	11	12	13
A	B	C	D	E	F	G	H	I	J	K	L	M

14	15	16	17	18	19	20	21	22	23	24	25	26
N	O	P	Q	R	S	T	U	V	W	X	Y	Z

F A T H E R, i
6 1 20 8 5 18 9

A M S O R R Y
1 13 19 15 18 18 25

F O R A L L
6 15 18 1 12 12

M Y S i N S.
13 25 19 9 14 19

How can
we return
to God?

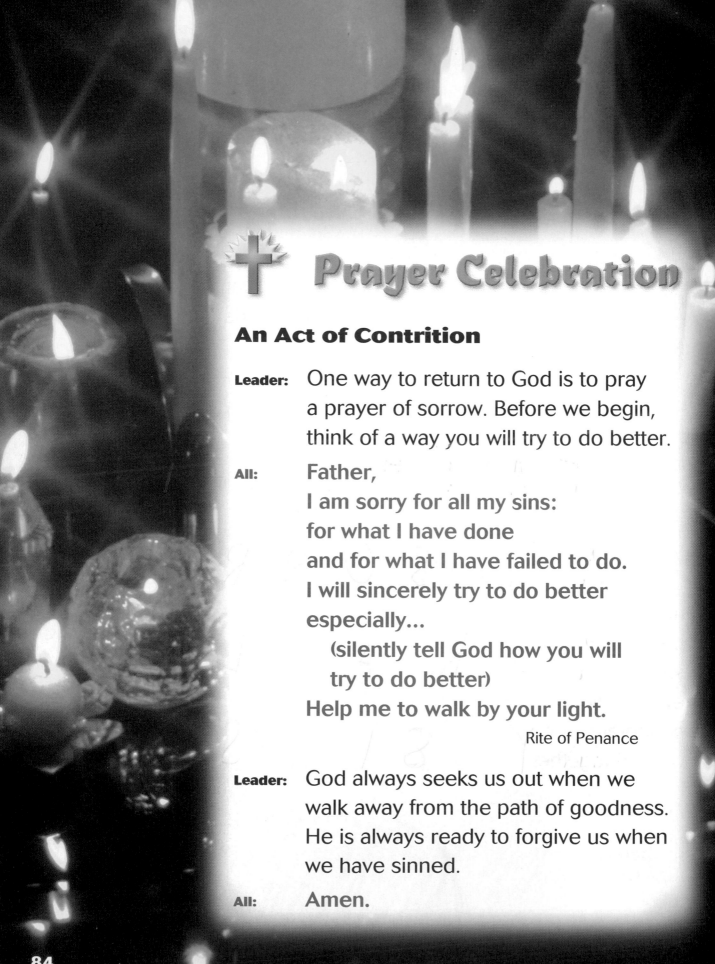

✝ Prayer Celebration

An Act of Contrition

Leader: One way to return to God is to pray a prayer of sorrow. Before we begin, think of a way you will try to do better.

All: Father,
I am sorry for all my sins:
for what I have done
and for what I have failed to do.
I will sincerely try to do better
especially...
   (silently tell God how you will
   try to do better)
Help me to walk by your light.

Rite of Penance

Leader: God always seeks us out when we walk away from the path of goodness. He is always ready to forgive us when we have sinned.

All: Amen.

WE CARE About Family and Friends

Pam Has a Problem

Pam Larsen is fourteen years old, Bobby is ten, and Sara is seven. Every Sunday, the Larsen family makes plans for the next week.

Last Sunday Bobby said, "Dad, I'll be coming home late on Tuesday. That's the day of our soccer game."

Sara said, "I need a ride after school on Friday, Mom. That's when I have my piano lesson."

Then Pam said, "I have a problem. For my school project, I will need to use our computer every day!"

Everybody in the family shares the computer. All of them talked about Pam's problem. Everybody agreed to let Pam use the computer whenever she needed it. Pam's problem was solved because everybody cooperated, or worked together.

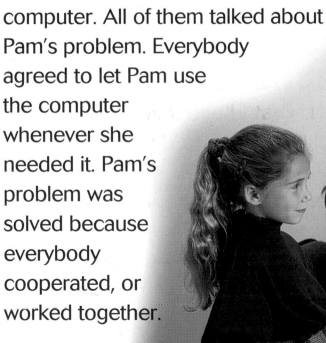

What does the word cooperate mean?

Think About It

What happens when people in the family cooperate? What happens when friends cooperate?

Circle the words that tell about how people feel when they cooperate.

(laugh)   angry

smile   cry

sad   happy

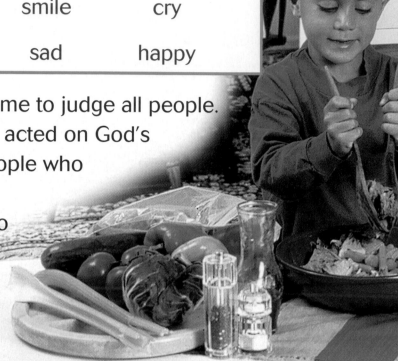

Learn About It

Jesus told us that he will come to judge all people. He will find the people who acted on God's word. Jesus will find the people who treated others fairly.

People in a family need to be fair with each other. Each person has rights. Each person has duties, too. To be fair, each person must respect the rights of all the others. Everybody needs to carry out their duties, too.

Do Something About It

What rights do you have in your family? What duties do you have?

Draw a picture of a way you cooperate at home.

Organizer

Read the words on the signs. Then write the word that completes each sentence.

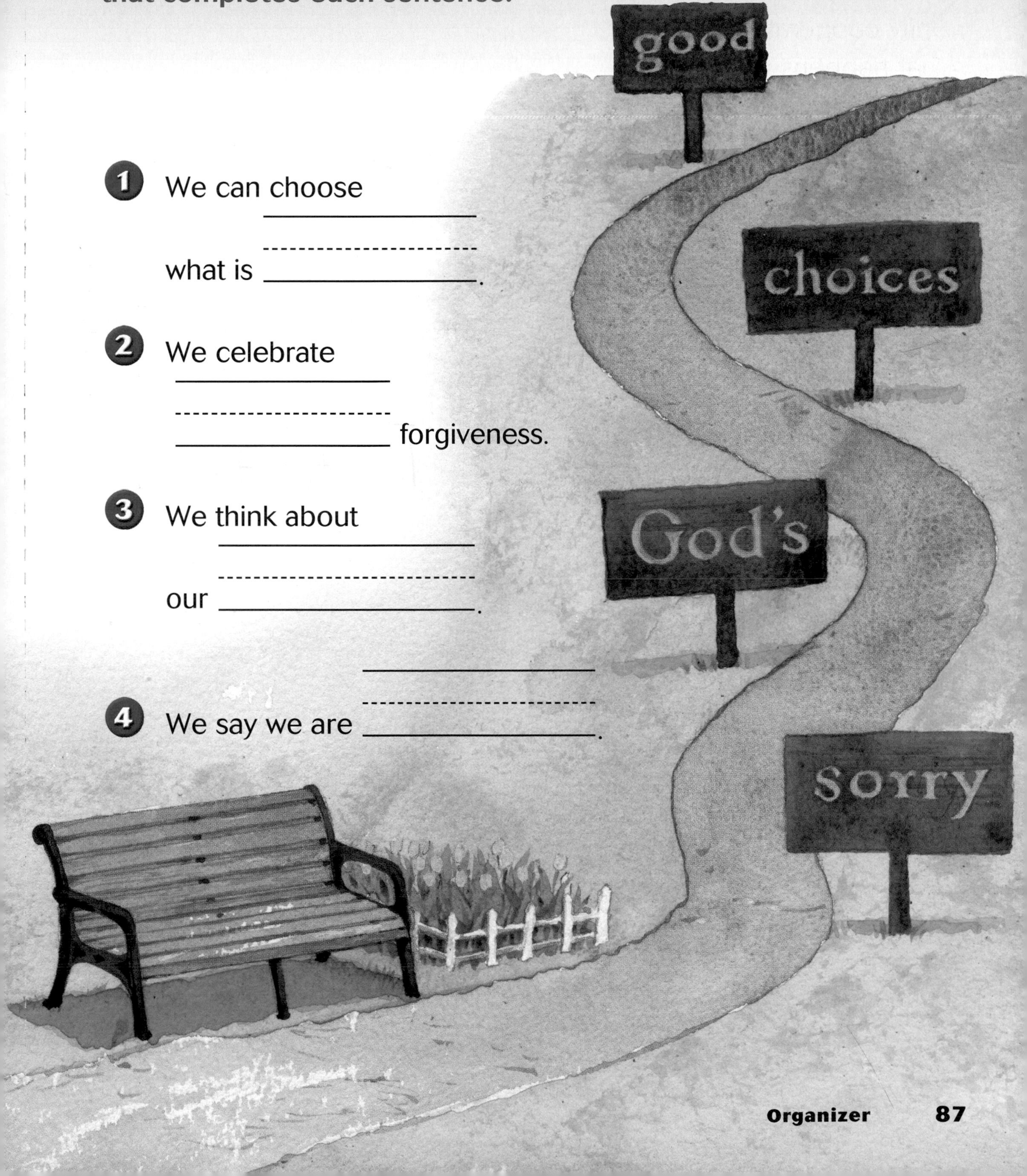

good

choices

God's

sorry

1 We can choose
_____
- -
what is _____.

2 We celebrate
_____
- -
_____ forgiveness.

3 We think about
_____
- -
our _____.

_____
- -
4 We say we are _____.

A Remember the story "The Forgiving Father." Then put the story in order. Write the numbers 1, 2, 3, 4, and 5 in the boxes.

[1] The boy moved far away from home.

[ ] The father gave money to the boy.

[5] They had a "welcome home" party.

[ ] The father forgave the boy.

[ ] The boy was sorry for his wrong choices.

B Circle the correct answer.

1. Our ____ tells us right from wrong.
   conscience   brain   idea

2. We ____ when we turn away from God.
   praise   spend   sin

3. God wants us to be ____ for our sins.
   sorry   polite   lonely

4. God lets us choose between right and wrong.
   This is called ____.
   conscience   prayer   free choice

C Use the words in the box to complete the sentences.

> healing grace God

1. The gift of God's _____ helps us stay away from sin.

2. Reconciliation is a sacrament of _____.

3. The forgiveness of _____ is called absolution.

D Draw a line to the word that completes each sentence.

1. The Ten Commandments are God's ____.   •   • mortal

2. The Ten Commandments help us make good ____.   •   • choices

3. Serious sins that separate us from our friendship with God are called ____ sins.   •   • laws

4. Less serious sins that weaken our friendship with God are called ____ sins.   •   • sins

5. Mistakes are never ____.   •   • venial

E Write the numbers 1 to 5 on the correct balloons.

1. Which balloon tells what separates us from God? Write **1** on it.

2. Which balloon tells who helps us do better when we are sorry for our sins? Write **2** on it.

3. Which balloon names the prayer we say to show we are sorry for our sins? Write **3** on it.

4. Which balloon tells about being sorry or sad about something? Write **4** on it.

5. Which balloon tells what God always does when we are sorry for our sins? Write **5** on it.

We Celebrate the Word of God

T he Word of God is Jesus Christ among us. When we listen to the Scripture readings, we are taught the way of the Gospel. We are inspired to live as true followers of Jesus.

> But some seed fell on rich soil, and produced fruit, a hundred or sixty or thirtyfold. Whoever has ears ought to hear.
>
> Matthew 13:8-9

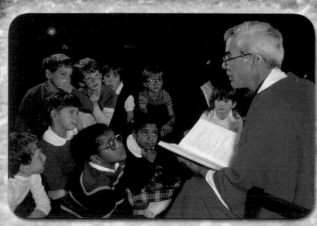

The farmer plants seeds that will grow into food. Like seeds, our faith grows when we listen to God's word.

Go and Listen

Words and Music by Robert J. Batastini

Cantor, All repeat

Go and lis - ten to the Word of God.

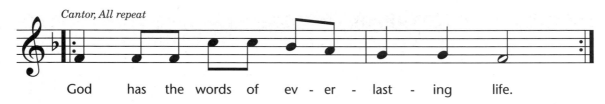

Cantor, All repeat

God has the words of ev - er - last - ing life.

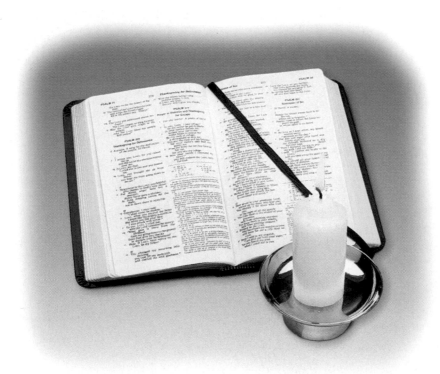

FAMILY TIME

A choice of things to do at home

We Learn About God's Love

The Bible is a book filled with many kinds of literature, such as stories, letters, prayers, and songs. The Bible tells of God's love for us, from the moment of creation on. This chapter encourages children to be aware of the Bible as a tool for learning about God's gift of creation, his love for us, and his gift of his Son, Jesus.

Biblical current events

Think of an event that has happened in your family and write about it in Biblical style. There are many styles to use as models: the letters of St. Paul, the psalms of David, a prophecy, or an adventure story similar to the one about Jonah and the whale.

Creating with clay

God made us out of clay, according to one account in Genesis. Together, take some clay and make something that represents your thanks to God for creating each family member and continuing to love you throughout your lives.

Who came first?

With the members of your family, make a simple Bible timeline. We all know that Jesus came after Moses. But did Abraham come before or after Moses? How about Esther or David? Have fun discussing what everyone knows about who came after whom in the Bible.

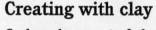

✝ **A Prayer for the Week**

In the creation story, Lord, we learn of your goodness. Thank you for loving all your creatures. Your works are wonderful, Lord. Amen.

FAMILY TIME

Something to Do . . .

On Sunday

Listen to the readings at Mass. Then, later in the day, choose one of the readings to discuss with your family.

Through the Week

As a family, think about the good parts of being a son, a daughter, or a parent. Say a prayer of thanksgiving for the role God plays in all your lives.

Visit Our Web Site

www.blestarewe.com

Something to Think About . . .

In the Hands of God

Can any of you by worrying add a single moment to your life-span?
Matthew 6:27

This Gospel story from Matthew is about God's love. Jesus tells it to people who are worried about having enough food and clothing. Jesus tells the people not to worry about these things. He asks the people to trust that God will care for them, just as he cares for the birds in the sky and the flowers in the field.

From this story we can understand that God takes care of everything—including us—and that we shouldn't spend our time worrying. By not worrying, we put our trust in God and show that we appreciate his loving care.

Something to Know About . . . Our Heritage in Art

The painstaking work of monks and artists of the Middle Ages has left us with some priceless treasures of Scriptures copied and illuminated by hand. *Illumination* is a kind of decoration that was often used to illustrate and highlight the first letter of a passage. Artists used bright colors and gold to intertwine pictures of flowers and animals in the letter, making it so fancy that it was sometimes difficult to figure out what letter it was supposed to be. But the artworks are extraordinarily detailed and beautiful. They show the reverence in which the artists held the Holy Scriptures.

9 We Learn About God's Love

God looked at everything he had made.
He found it very good.

Based on Genesis 1:31

Share

The earth that God created has many kinds of land and water. It has mountains, forests, and deserts. It has rivers, lakes, and oceans.

The earth has many kinds of plants and animals, too. Name some plants and animals you know about.

Draw a picture that shows your favorite part of God's creation.

What does creation tell us about God?

✠ God Loves All Creation

One day, Jesus told his followers this story about God's love.

"Some people worry about what they will eat and drink. Other people worry about what clothes to wear. But I say, do not worry. Instead, look at the birds in the sky. God takes good care of them. Look at the flowers in the field. God takes good care of them, too.

"So have faith. God loves you even more than the birds and flowers. God is a loving Father. You are his sons and daughters. God knows what you need. He will always take care of you."

Based on Matthew 6:25–34

Ways We Learn About God

The story Jesus told about God taking good care of all that he created is in the **Bible**. The Bible is also called **Scripture**. We learn about God's love for us from the Bible and from the teachings of Jesus.

Our Church Teaches

God is the creator of all things. We read the **word of God** in the Bible.

Jesus is the **Son of God**. We read the teachings of Jesus in the Bible.

Faith Words

Bible
The Bible is the word of God.

Son of God
Son of God is a special title for Jesus. Jesus is God's only Son.

How can people show love for God's creation?

Respond

Caring for God's Creation

The Sisters of Earth are taking care of God's creation. Most of the Sisters of Earth are religious sisters. They want to heal the earth and protect it. Some Sisters of Earth live on farms, where they take care of the land. Others teach college students about farming, gardening, and caring for the earth. Others help people recycle things that can be used again.

 How can you care for God's creation?

Activities

1. Learn to sign the words "God cares for you."

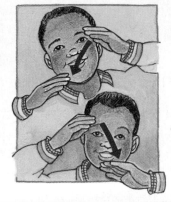

| God | cares for | you. |

2. Think of something God made that begins with each letter in the word <u>creation</u>. Write the words on the lines. The first one has been done for you.

Clouds

Racoons

Earth

A

T

I

O

N

How can the Bible help us celebrate God's love?

Prayer Celebration

Bible Prayer

Celebrate the gifts of God's creation with this prayer of praise from the Bible. When you pray "O God, you are great indeed," lift your arms high, with the palms facing up.

Reader 1: You have made the clouds and wind.

All: O God, you are great indeed!

Reader 2: You have made the birds and trees.

All: O God, you are great indeed!

Reader 3: You have made the lakes and mountains.

All: O God, you are great indeed!

Reader 4: You have made the land and seas.

All: O God, you are great indeed!

Reader 5: How can we celebrate God's love?

All: We will sing praise to God.

Based on Psalm 104

FAMILY TIME

A choice of things to do at home

We Listen to God's Word

In this chapter, children will come to realize that when we hear the Scripture readings, we are listening to God's word. The children will learn the responses said during the Liturgy of the Word. They will also learn that the Nicene Creed is a prayer that states the beliefs that Catholics hold.

What is it for?

Assemble a group of varied reading materials, such as a newspaper, television guide, dictionary, math textbook, photo album, and Bible. Ask each family member to choose one item and describe its purpose. The Bible should be described as a holy book that contains stories about God's love for us.

Good listening

As a family, discuss ways to be a good listener. Create a chart to list the ideas. These may include being quiet, looking at the person who is speaking, and not talking until the person is finished. Decorate your chart and display it.

A Prayer for the Week

Lord, we lift up our hearts, our minds, and our ears to your word. Help us understand your Scriptures. Give us the gift of understanding, Lord. Amen.

Good news

Put a "Remember the Good News!" sign on your refrigerator. Tell each other some good news this week. This will prepare your child to learn about the "Good News" of the Gospels.

FAMILY TIME

Something to Do . . .

On Sunday

Show your child the Old and New Testaments in the Bible. Point out that the New Testament contains the Gospel stories that tell about Jesus.

Through the Week

Read aloud some Bible passages. End your readings with the responses used at Mass.

Visit Our Web Site

 www.blestarewe.com

Something to Think About . . .

The Sower and the Seed

Whoever has ears ought to hear.
Matthew 13:9

The Parable of the Sower that Jesus tells is about the importance of really hearing God's word and understanding it. Jesus equates the seeds the sower scatters with God's word. He categorizes people as those who hear God's word but don't understand it; those who hear God's word but believe it for only a short time; those who hear God's word but don't focus on it; or those who hear God's word and understand it. Jesus is saying that it is one thing to listen and hear, but we must also understand and act. This is what leads to Christian growth.

Something to Know About . . .

Our Heritage in Church Design

Catholic churches usually have a crucifix, statues, a baptismal font, an altar, and a lectern. The lectern reminds us that God speaks to us. A lectern may also be called an ambo. Starting around the ninth century, churches had two stands, called ambos. One was for Gospel readings and one was for readings from the letters. The one for the Gospel became more and more ornate until, by the thirteenth century, it became known as the pulpit. The word *pulpit* comes from the Latin *pulpitum*, meaning "stage." These ornate pulpits were at first built in Italian churches. Over time, they have been made in many styles and materials, such as stone and iron.

10 We Listen to God's Word

Listening to God's word is like building a house on rock.
A house like that will not fall down.

Based on Matthew 7:24–25

Share

Most people like hearing a good story. The story can be funny, sad, or even scary. To enjoy a story, we need to be good listeners.

1. Who is the best storyteller you know?

_____

_____

_____

2. What story do you like to listen to again and again?

_____

_____

_____

3. Why do you like this story?

_____

_____

_____

_____

When do church members listen to the stories of Jesus?

Hear & Believe

✝ A Story About Listening

One day, Jesus told this story about listening to God's word.

"A farmer scattered seeds in his field. Some seeds fell on the path. Birds ate them up. Some seeds fell on rocks. The seeds dried up and died. Some seeds fell among weeds. The weeds grew up with the seeds and choked them. Other seeds fell on good soil. They took root, grew, and produced good fruit.

"People are like the different places where the farmer's seeds fell. Some people hear God's word but do not try to understand it. Some people hear God's word but only remember it for a short time. They are like the rocks. Some people hear God's word in church but then forget about it the rest of the week. They are like the ground that has many weeds. Other people hear God's word and really listen to it. They are like the good soil. Faith grows in them."

Based on Matthew 13:1–9, 18–23

104

Listening to God's Word

The Bible story tells us that when we really listen to God's word, our faith grows. At Mass we come together to listen to God's word from the Bible. This part of the Mass is the **Liturgy of the Word**.

Our Church Teaches

During the Liturgy of the Word on Sunday, we listen to three readings. The third reading is the **Gospel**. It tells the story of Jesus' life. Then the priest or deacon gives a talk called the homily. The **homily** helps us understand the Bible readings. After the Gospel and the homily, we state what Catholics believe in a prayer called the **Nicene Creed**.

GO TO page 6 to pray the Nicene Creed.

Faith Words

Nicene Creed Catholics tell what they believe when they pray the Nicene Creed at Mass. The creed tells about God's love for us and about how Jesus saved us.

How can we show we are listening during the Liturgy of the Word?

Respond
We Take Part at Mass

Jill loves Jesus. She wants to learn more about his life and teachings. That is why she tries her best to take part in Mass. She sings songs with other parish members. She answers "Amen" to the prayers. She stands, sits, and kneels with everyone else. And she listens to the Bible readings. She says the response at the end of each reading.

After the first Bible reading and after the second Bible reading, the reader says, "The Word of the Lord."

Jill answers, "Thanks be to God."

After the Gospel reading, the priest or deacon says, "The Gospel of the Lord."

Jill answers, "Praise to you, Lord Jesus Christ."

Then Jill sits down to listen to the homily.

Activity

What word is missing in each sentence?

1. The first part of Mass is the Liturgy of the _word_.

2. After the first reading we say, "_Thanks_ be to God."

3. The _____ tells the good news about Jesus' life and teachings.

4. After the Gospel we say, "_____ to you, Lord Jesus Christ."

5. The talk given by the priest or deacon is called the _____.

6. The Nicene _____ is a prayer about what we believe as Catholics.

Now do the puzzle. Find and circle the missing words.

A	C	B	E	C	F	H	G
I	W	J	K	R	L	T	M
G	O	S	P	E	L	H	N
O	R	P	Q	E	R	A	S
U	D	T	V	D	X	N	Y
H	O	M	I	L	Y	K	Z
B	A	P	R	A	I	S	E

How can we celebrate with a prayer song?

Prayer Celebration

Praying with a Psalm

After the first reading at Mass, we respond with a special prayer-song. This part of the Liturgy of the Word is called the responsorial psalm.

Pray this responsorial psalm together.

Reader 1: The seed that falls on good ground will yield a fruitful harvest.

All: **The seed that falls on good ground will yield a fruitful harvest.**

Reader 2: Our God, you take care of the earth and send rain to help the soil grow all kinds of crops.

All: **The seed that falls on good ground will yield a fruitful harvest.**

Reader 3: Your rivers never run dry, and you prepare the earth to produce much grain.

All: **The seed that falls on good ground will yield a fruitful harvest.**

Lectionary for Masses with Children

FAMILY TIME

A choice of things to do at home

We Act on God's Word

Jesus made the treatment of other human beings the focus of his time on earth. How we should think about and respond to others was the topic of many of Jesus' teachings. He gave us many examples of service. Children need to understand that Jesus cared for others to show his love for God. Jesus wants us to do the same by helping and serving others.

Followers of Jesus

Think of people who showed their love for others. Mother Teresa showed her love, especially for the poor of India. Dr. Martin Luther King Jr. showed his love for those who were not treated fairly by others. Mahatma Gandhi, who was deeply influenced by the New Testament, showed his love for those who treated each other peacefully. With your child, make a medal out of construction paper to honor any person you know who follows Jesus. Write the person's name and the words *Follower of Jesus* on the medal.

Hear no evil

Treating others well involves the way we speak about them and the things we listen to about them. Help your child and yourself avoid gossip. Don't talk negatively or listen to negative talk about others. Instead, help others and speak positively about them.

A quality person

Those who behave toward others as Jesus did have certain qualities in common. What are some of these qualities? Do you see these in your family? Discuss the qualities that make a good person.

✝ A Prayer for the Week

Dear Jesus, give us the grace and strength to follow you. Help us trust as you did, love as you did, and care for others as you did. We trust you to help us. Amen.

FAMILY TIME

Something to Do . . .

On Sunday

What do today's readings tell you about being a good person? Pick one message from the homily to take home from this week's liturgy.

Through the Week

Using Jesus as your model, pick one thing that he did and try to make it part of your life.

Visit Our Web Site

 www.blestarewe.com

Something to Know About . . .

Our Heritage in Literature

Thomas Merton was a Catholic monk who died in 1968. He was a convert to Catholicism as a young adult and wrote an autobiography in 1948 about how he moved from atheism to Catholicism. That book, *The Seven Storey Mountain*, became the most famous memoir ever written by an American Catholic. He was a social activist and spoke out on such topics as racial justice, violence, and world peace. His clear vision of how to live a Christian life, his wonderful writing, and his ever-questioning spirit are inspirations for those who have come after him.

Something to Think About . . .

In Loving Service

Amen, I say to you, whatever you did for one of these least brothers of mine, you did for me.
Matthew 25:40

The standard of behavior that Jesus sets for us is very high. He expects us to love and care for our family members, our friends, and even people we do not like. Jesus treated everyone with love and wants us to do the same.

In the Gospel story, Jesus told about the works of mercy. The works of mercy include feeding the hungry, giving drink to the thirsty, sheltering the homeless, clothing the naked, and visiting the sick and those in prison. Jesus is saying that when we help others in loving service, we show our love for God. We are challenged daily to treat all people with love.

11 The Act on God's Word

If you believe in me, you will act as
I have acted.

Based on John 14:12

Share

So many actions
That we take.
We walk and ride.
We bake a cake.

So many actions
Every day.
We laugh and smile.
We learn and pray.

Imagine yourself in each
picture. What would you do?
Write about an action
you would take.

I would

_____

- -

_____ .

I would

_____

- - - - - - - - - - - - - - - - - - - -

_____ .

How can
we act on
God's word?

Hear & Believe

How Christians Act

Jesus told his followers, "I will return to earth at the end of time. Then I will judge all the people in the world. I will put the people in two groups. To the first group I will say, 'You have done well. I invite you to stay with me forever.' But I will tell the second group, 'Go far away. I don't want to see you again.'"

The people in the first group had treated everyone the same way as they would have treated Jesus. They gave food to the hungry. They gave drink to people who were thirsty. They made new people feel at home. They shared their own clothes with people who needed them. They cared for the sick. And they visited people in prison.

The first group of people had acted on God's word. That is why Jesus will welcome them to be with him forever.

Based on Matthew 25:31–46

Responding in Action

Jesus did good things because he loved God and wanted to please him. Jesus wants his followers to respond to God's word, too. Jesus wants us to treat others with love.

Our Church Teaches

Jesus told his followers about some good actions. They are called the **works of mercy**. When we help others in loving **service**, we act as Jesus did.

The Works of Mercy

Feed the hungry.

Give drink to the thirsty.

Shelter the homeless.

Give clothing to the poor.

Visit the sick.

Visit those in prison.

Pray for those who have died.

We Believe

Jesus shows us how to act on God's word. He teaches us that by loving our neighbor, we show our love for God.

Faith Words

works of mercy
The works of mercy tell how Jesus wants us to help others.

service
Service means doing work that helps others.

How can we act like Jesus?

Respond

Saint Martin de Porres

Martin lived a long time ago in Peru, South America. Martin wanted to spend his life acting on God's word. So he became a brother who worked for the Church. No job was too big for Martin. And no job was too little. Martin served God in everything he did.

What did Martin do? Sometimes he cut the hair of the other brothers. Sometimes he brought food and medicine to the sick. He helped find homes for orphans. He gave food and clothing to poor people. Martin was especially kind to people no one else loved.

"Why do you do these things?" the people asked him.

"I see the face of Jesus in everyone," Martin said. "When I show love to people, I am showing love to Jesus."

? What does Saint Martin's story tell us about loving others?

Activity

Follow the directions on the path.

Write one way that Martin acted as Jesus did.

I dan't

Draw about a time that you acted as Jesus did.

Act out a scene about one of these works of mercy.

Visit the sick.
Feed the hungry.

If you could add a work of mercy to the list, what would it be?

Write it on the sign below.

How can we celebrate acting on God's word?

Prayer Celebration

A Saint's Prayer

Saint Frances Cabrini and some friends in Italy became famous for teaching children, caring for orphans, and helping the sick. Mother Cabrini was asked to come to the United States to help the many poor people who had come here from Italy. She directed the building of schools, orphanages, and hospitals. Mother Cabrini spent her life acting on God's word and helping others.

Listen to this prayer. It is based on a prayer that Mother Cabrini wrote.

Lord, you have made me see so many things.
I see that you are the one who acts.
You are the one who does everything.
I can do nothing without you.
You are the one who does all.
I stand in wonder
of your great and beautiful works.

Now read the prayer aloud together.

FAMILY TIME

A choice of things to do at home

We Pray for Others

In this chapter, children will become more aware of the needs of others. Sometimes all we can do to help others is to pray for them. The children will come to realize that, when we pray, we trust God to care for people's needs. The children will also compose their own prayers for other people.

Trust walk

Blindfold one family member. Then have someone be the trust-walk leader. It is the leader's job to make sure that the blindfolded person doesn't bump into anything or get hurt. It is the blindfolded person's job to trust the leader. Take turns being the blindfolded person and the leader. Then talk about what it was like to play these roles.

Butterfly house

In order to survive, winter butterflies either migrate or hibernate. To help the ones that hibernate, you and your child can put a box with slits in it outdoors. Kits are available in hobby stores for building butterfly houses. It's a way to help some of God's fragile creatures.

What's wrong?

With your child, practice solving a pretend or real problem, such as making up with a friend or finding time to do homework. First, state the problem. Next, propose and discuss possible solutions. Finally, decide on the best solution.

A Prayer for the Week

Lord, sometimes we are caught up with our own needs and we ignore the needs of those around us. Open our hearts to see the needs of others. Amen.

Something to Do . . .

On Sunday

Listen for the priest to say the words "Let us pray." When he pauses, use the opportunity to be quiet and prayerful. When he continues, listen with attentive ears and an open heart.

Through the Week

Take time each day to quiet yourself and pray for the needs of others.

Visit Our Web Site

 www.blestarewe.com

Something to Know About . . .

Our Heritage in Prayer

Do not despise my poor prayer. Do not let my trust be confounded!

The prayer above is part of a novena to Saint Jude, the patron saint of impossible causes. A novena is a repeated prayer asking for a specific intention. *Novena* comes from the Latin word *novem*, or *nine*. Most novenas are said nine times in a row for nine days in a row. Often said as a last resort by the desperate or the hopeless, novenas may be made to saints, to angels, and to God himself. Mary, the mother of Jesus, is perhaps the person most often addressed in this form of devotion.

Something to Think About . . .

Praying for Ourselves and Others

ask and it will be given to you; seek and you will find; knock and the door will be opened to you.
Matthew 7:7

Just as Jesus told his friends and followers to trust God, so he tells us to do the same. Jesus taught that God gives us what we need when we pray. He also said to pray for the needs of others. As Christians we pray for our needs in prayers called *petitions*. God gives us the support and strength to deal with whatever comes our way. When we pray for the needs of others, the prayers are called *intercessions*. We often pray for those we love, since we know their needs. We trust God to care for others when we pray for them.

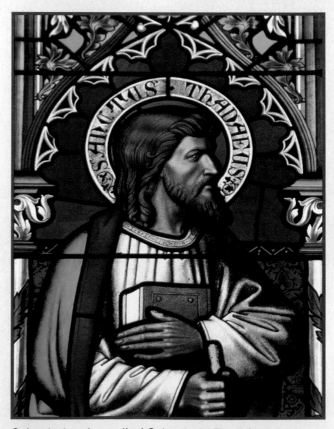

Saint Jude, also called Saint Jude Thaddeus

12 We Pray for Others

 O God, hear me and answer my prayer.

Based on Psalm 17:6

Share

Have you ever made a list of things you wish you could do? Perhaps you want to learn to ice skate. Maybe you would like to see the ocean.

Write three of your wishes here.

My Wish List

1. I wish _____ .

2. I wish _____ .

3. I wish _____ .

 What do church members ask for when they pray?

✝ Jesus and Prayer

On the night before he died, Jesus ate dinner with his friends. After dinner, Jesus prayed for his friends. "Father, please help my friends in their work. Help them tell others about your love."

Jesus taught about different kinds of prayer. One time, Jesus said we should ask God for what we need for ourselves. "Ask, and you shall receive," Jesus said. "Pray for what you need, and God will give it to you."

Another time, Jesus said we should pray for the needs of other people. "When you come together to pray for others, I will be with you," Jesus promised. "God will give you whatever you ask for in my name."

Based on John 17:9–21; Matthew 7:7–8; 18:19–20; John 16:23

Christian Prayer

Jesus told his friends to place their trust in God. When we pray for ourselves, we know that God will answer us. When we pray for other people, we trust that God will care for them.

Our Church Teaches

As Christians we pray for our own needs. We call these prayers petitions. We ask God to give us what we need to be good followers of Jesus.

We also pray for the needs of others. We call these prayers intercessions. At Mass the Liturgy of the Word ends with the **Prayer of the Faithful**. In this prayer of intercession, we pray for people everywhere.

We Believe

We trust our heavenly Father to answer our prayers. We know that God loves us and gives us what is truly good for us.

Faith Words

Prayer of the Faithful
The Prayer of the Faithful is the last part of the Liturgy of the Word at Mass. During this prayer we pray for ourselves and for people everywhere.

How can we pray a prayer of intercession?

121

Respond
The Needs of Others

Before we can pray for others, we need to know what they need. The photos on this page tell stories. Talk about what the people need.

❓ How would you ask God to care for these people?

Activities

The prayer below is a prayer for people in need.
> For those who are sick,
> we pray to the Lord.

1. Use your own words to complete these prayers for other people.

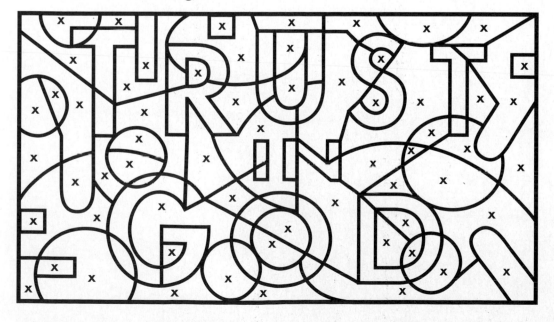

For those who _____,

we pray to the Lord.

For those who _____,

we pray to the Lord.

2. Color each space that has an **X**. What is the hidden message?

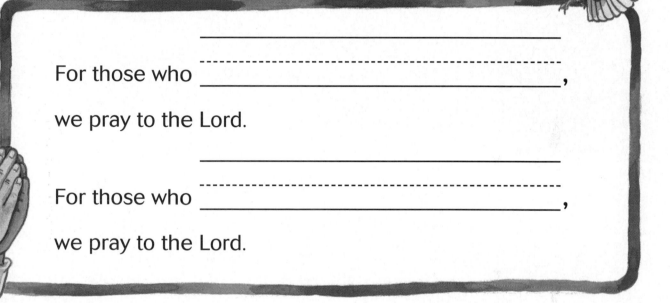

How can we celebrate a Prayer of the Faithful?

✝ Prayer Celebration

Prayer of the Faithful

During the Prayer of the Faithful, we remember that God is the Father of everyone in the world. We care about others because they are like our brothers and sisters.

Pray this Prayer of the Faithful.

Reader 1: For all the people in the world. May they know God's love, we pray to the Lord.

All: **Lord, hear our prayer.**

Reader 2: For church members throughout the world. May they follow Jesus by loving one another, we pray to the Lord.

All: **Lord, hear our prayer.**

Reader 3: For world leaders. May they make good choices so that all people may live in peace, we pray to the Lord.

All: **Lord, hear our prayer.**

Reader 4: For those who are hungry, and poor, and homeless, we pray to the Lord.

All: **Lord, hear our prayer.**

Partners in Planting

Father Garcia found something out about the senior citizens in the parish. It seems that many of them wanted to have a garden! A friend of Father Garcia's let these older people use some empty land. Now they had a place to plant their gardens.

But gardening is very hard work. So Father Garcia asked some religious education students to help. Each student became a partner with an older gardener. They became friends. The children learned so many things! First, they learned to respect their partners. But most of all, they learned to respect God's wonderful creation!

What have you learned from a senior citizen?

Think About It

Do you know anyone who has a vegetable garden or a flower garden? Do they like taking care of it?

What is your favorite vegetable or flower? Draw a picture of it.

Learn About It

The Earth that God has given us is a wonderful place. But God tells us we must respect the Earth. We must take care of it. We must use it well.

Today many children live in cities. It is not easy to learn to respect the Earth in a city. Mostly you see roads, parking lots, and buildings. The children in Father Garcia's parish are lucky. They have the vegetable gardens. And they have older people to teach them how to respect our Earth.

Do Something About It

You may not have a garden. But you can still learn to respect the Earth.

Use a ✔ to show things you could do to respect our Earth:

☐ pick up litter   ☐ grow plants outdoors

☐ recycle plastic   ☐ throw cans on the grass

Use these words to complete the sentences.

pray   love   act   listen

1 In the Bible we learn about God's
_____

_____ .

2 In the Bible we learn to
_____

_____ to God's word.

3 In the Bible we learn how to
_____

_____ on God's word.

4 We learn we must
_____

_____ for others.

A Remember the story "God Loves All Creation."
Then draw a circle around each correct answer.

1. Jesus said that God is a loving Father.　　**Yes　No**

2. Jesus wants us to worry a lot.　　**Yes　No**

3. God loves flowers more than he loves us.　　**Yes　No**

4. God will always take care of us.　　**Yes　No**

B Trace the dotted letters. Then fill in the missing letters.

1. God made all creation ___g___ o ____ d.

2. The B ____ b l ___e___ is the word of God.

3. Jesus is God's only S ___o___ ____.

4. God wants us to k ___n___ ow, l ___o___ ____ e,

    and ___S___ er ____ e him.

a. homily

b. Bible

c. Liturgy of the Word

d. Nicene Creed

C Read the words on the church. Circle the correct letter for each answer.

1. What is the part of the Mass when we listen to the readings called?   a   b   c   d

2. Where do the readings come from?   a   b   c   d

3. What is the talk that explains the Bible readings called?   a   b   c   d

4. What prayer at Mass says what Catholics believe?   a   b   c   d

D Draw a line from each reading at Mass to our response.

1. the first Bible reading   ●   ● Praise to you, Lord Jesus Christ.

2. the second Bible reading ●   ● Thanks be to God.

3. the Gospel   ●   ● Thanks be to God.

Review

E Draw a line under each sentence that names a work of mercy.

Feed the hungry.   **Take many naps.**

Play in the park.   **Visit the sick.**

F Use a ✔ to mark the sentences that are true.

☐ **1.** Saint Martin de Porres never acted on God's word.

☐ **2.** Martin saw the face of Jesus in everyone.

☐ **3.** Saint Frances Cabrini helped others.

☐ **4.** Mother Cabrini came from Italy.

G Write the correct answer on the line.

1. Work that helps others is _____.
   praise   service   creation

2. A petition is a kind of _____.
   song   reading   prayer

3. The Prayer of the Faithful is part of the

   _____

   _____.

   Mass   Bible   Church

We Celebrate the Gift of Eucharist

God's greatest gift to us is his only Son, Jesus Christ. We celebrate the Eucharist to praise and thank God for this gift. We celebrate to share more fully in the life of Christ.

*I am the bread of life.
Those who eat this bread
will never be hungry.*

Based on John 6:35

Jesus was buried in a tomb very much like the one shown here. We remember Jesus' death and Resurrection each time we receive Holy Communion.

Eat This Bread

John 6, Adapted by Robert J. Batastini and the Taizé Community

Music by Jacques Berthier

REFRAIN

Eat this bread, drink this cup, come to him and nev-er be hun - gry.

Eat this bread, drink this cup, trust in him and you will not thirst.

© 1984, Les Presses de Taizé, GIA Publications, Inc., agent.

FAMILY TIME

A choice of things to do at home

Jesus Saves Us from Sin

We know that Jesus gave up his life to save all of us from sin. We all share the benefit of his great sacrifice. This chapter presents the story of Jesus' death and Resurrection. Children will consider the concept of sacrifice as it applies to everyday life, and they will learn about the ultimate sacrifice made by Jesus when he gave up his life so that we could be saved from sin.

Gift giving

Help your child write a brief description of something (such as a handcrafted item or a picture) that could be made as a gift for a friend. The description should tell why the friend would like the gift. Then help your child make the item.

It's a sacrifice

Discuss the meaning of sacrifice by using an example, such as a sacrifice fly in baseball. Explain that sacrifice is the act of giving up one thing for the sake of something else. Help your child think of some advantages in making sacrifices.

The rugged cross

Together, make a cross of twigs held together with a piece of twine or a pipe cleaner. Display your work in a prominent place. Let it serve as a reminder that Jesus sacrificed his life to save us from sin.

✝ A Prayer for the Week

Your cross is a sign of your gift to us, O God. You gave the life of your Son, Jesus, so that we would be saved from sin. Amen.

FAMILY TIME

Something to Do . . .

On Sunday

After the consecration, say (or sing) the words "Christ has died, Christ is risen, Christ will come again" with a new sense of appreciation.

Through the Week

In gratitude for the gift of salvation that Jesus gave us, praise and thank God in prayers throughout each day.

Visit Our Web Site

www.blestarewe.com

Something to Think About . . .

The Greatest Gift

Having bought a linen cloth, he took him down, wrapped him in the linen cloth and laid him in a tomb that had been hewn out of the rock.
Mark 15:46

 Jesus loved us so much that he accepted a punishment for a crime he had not committed. Jesus sacrificed his life when he died on the cross. He gave us the gift of his life, and it all stemmed from his love. Jesus is God's greatest gift to us. His Resurrection from the dead to new life is central to our faith. He is our Savior, having saved us from sin and given us everlasting life. How blessed we are to have received such a love!

Something to Know About . . . Our Heritage

Many have been inspired by God's raising Jesus to glory. One person was a French priest named Basil Anthony Moreau. He was born in 1799, at the end of the French Revolution. The country was devastated, and many people were needed to minister. Father Moreau gathered a group of priests and brothers and established the Congregation of Holy Cross in 1837. Today there are four Holy Cross congregations who follow the spirit and ministry of Father Moreau: the Congregation of Holy Cross (priests and brothers), the Marianites of Holy Cross, the Sisters of the Holy Cross, and the Sisters of Holy Cross. All of these groups conduct ministries around the world.

13 Jesus Saves Us from Sin

The greatest love you can show is to give up your life for your friends.

Based on John 15:13

Share

Acting on God's word is not always easy. Sometimes we have to give up what we want. Sometimes we have to put the needs of others first.

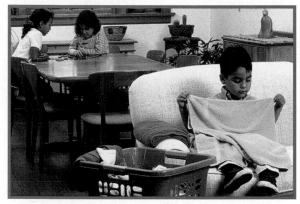

What is the boy giving up?

Why is he doing this?

What is the girl giving up?

Why is she doing this?

Draw a picture that shows a time when you gave up something.

What did Jesus give up for us?

✝ Jesus Gives Up His Life

Jesus gave up his life to save us from sin. On the night before he died, Jesus was arrested by his enemies. The next day, soldiers led Jesus to a place where they nailed him to a large wooden cross. Then they waited for Jesus to die.

After Jesus died, some of his friends took him away and buried him.

Three days later Jesus' friends went to visit his grave, or tomb. When they got there, Jesus was gone. An angel told the friends that Jesus had been raised from the dead.

Based on Mark 15:1–47; 16:1–6

God's Gift of Jesus

Jesus is God's greatest gift to us. Jesus gave up his life as a **sacrifice** for our sins. A sacrifice is a special gift that is given out of love.

We call Jesus our **Savior**. A savior is someone who rescues others from danger. Jesus saves us from sin and death.

Our Church Teaches

Jesus died on the cross to save us from our sins. Three days later, God raised Jesus to new life. By his life, death, and **Resurrection**, Jesus showed us God's love.

We Believe

Jesus' Resurrection is an important belief of our faith. Because of our Savior's Resurrection, we are saved from sin and given everlasting life.

Faith Words

sacrifice
A sacrifice is a special gift that is given out of love.

Resurrection
Resurrection is Jesus' being raised from the dead to new life.

How can we show love through sacrifice?

137

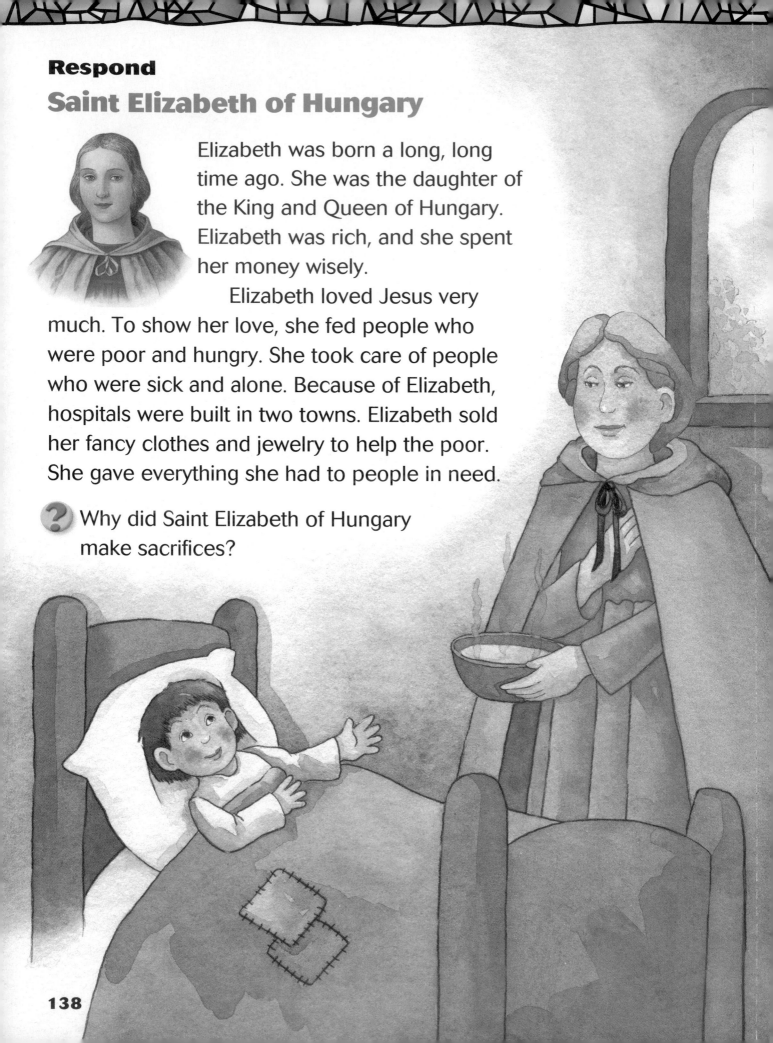

Respond
Saint Elizabeth of Hungary

Elizabeth was born a long, long time ago. She was the daughter of the King and Queen of Hungary. Elizabeth was rich, and she spent her money wisely.

Elizabeth loved Jesus very much. To show her love, she fed people who were poor and hungry. She took care of people who were sick and alone. Because of Elizabeth, hospitals were built in two towns. Elizabeth sold her fancy clothes and jewelry to help the poor. She gave everything she had to people in need.

? Why did Saint Elizabeth of Hungary make sacrifices?

Activities

1. Think of one sacrifice you could make this week. Write about how this sacrifice will show your love for someone.

   _____

   -

   _____

   _____

   -

   _____

   _____

   -

   _____

2. At Mass we listen as the priest prays, "Let us proclaim the mystery of faith."

Trace over the dotted words below. You will find "the mystery of faith."

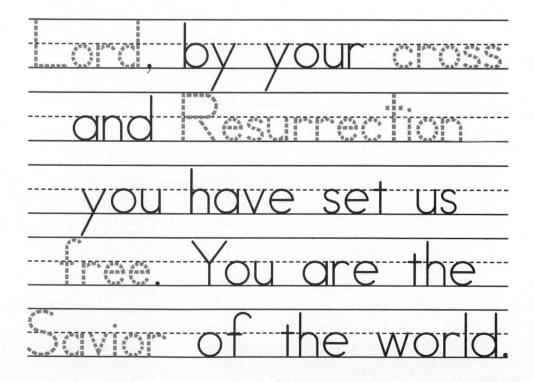

Lord, by your cross and Resurrection you have set us free. You are the Savior of the world.

How can we celebrate the sacrifice of Jesus?

✝ Prayer Celebration

A Prayer of Faith

During the Mass, we remember that Jesus died and was raised from the dead. We pray:

Christ has died,

Christ is risen,

Christ will come again.

FAMILY TIME

A choice of things to do at home

We Receive the Gift of Jesus

Some gifts are so great that we remember them for a lifetime. Other gifts, such as fresh air and clean water, we hardly give any thought to at all. This chapter presents the concept of Jesus in the Eucharist as gift.

Children will learn that we remember the Last Supper at Mass. They will discover that Jesus is present in the bread and wine. Lastly, they will learn how to receive Jesus in the Eucharist.

It's all set

Teach your child how to set the table. Show where to put the plates, glasses, napkins, and silverware. If possible, put candles and flowers on the table. Explain that, just as the altar is set in a particular way for Mass, so the family table should be set for a meal.

A dinner to remember

Talk about some memorable meals that you and your child have eaten together. Who ate with you? Was it the food, the company, or the conversation that made these meals so special?

Eucharist word web

Make a word web for Eucharist. In the middle of a piece of paper, draw a circle big enough to write the word Eucharist inside. Then draw lines out from the circle and write and circle words that your child associates with Eucharist, such as *Jesus*, *bread*, *wine*, and *church*.

✝ A Prayer for the Week

Thank you for the gift of Eucharist, Lord. We believe that you are truly present and that you give us forgiveness, life, and peace. Amen.

FAMILY TIME

Something to Do . . .

On Sunday

Listen carefully to the words of consecration. As you receive communion, think about what you have heard.

Through the Week

Find times to say, "My Lord and my God." This prayer will remind you of receiving Jesus in the Eucharist.

Visit Our Web Site

 www.blestarewe.com

Something to Know About . . .

Our Heritage in Music

Jesus Christ Superstar is a rock opera about the life of Christ with music by Andrew Lloyd Webber and lyrics by Tim Rice. The story is about the last week of Jesus' life, and it tells about the guilt Judas experiences when he betrays Jesus. The scene that depicts the Last Supper recreates the relationship of Jesus with the Twelve Apostles.

Originally performed on Broadway in 1971, the show ran from 1972 to 1980 in London. It opened on Broadway again in April, 2000. *Jesus Christ Superstar*, the first musical to incorporate rock music, gives us an opportunity to take a new look at a very familiar story and think about it in a fresh way.

Something to Think About . . .

The Body and Blood of Christ

While they were eating, Jesus took bread, said the blessing, broke it, and giving it to his disciples said, "Take and eat; this is my body."
Matthew 26:26

The Liturgy of the Eucharist is a memorial that makes present the sacrifice of Christ. Jesus is here with us as he was with his disciples at the Last Supper.

If we want to be close to Jesus, there is no better way than to receive communion. In the Eucharist the Holy Spirit changes the bread and wine into the Body and Blood of Christ. After receiving communion, we offer a prayer of thanks to show that we do not take Jesus' gift for granted.

14 We Receive the Gift of Jesus

I am the bread of life. Those who eat this bread will never be hungry.

Based on John 6:35

Share

We all need food and water to stay healthy. But we have other needs, or hungers, too. Look at these pictures. How is each person hungry?

Rosemary is very, very tired. She is hungry for

_____

- -

_____ .

Matt has not eaten since lunch. He is hungry for

_____

- -

_____ .

Luis can't rake all these leaves. He is hungry for

_____

- -

_____ .

How does Jesus answer our needs and hungers?

The Gift of Eucharist

At Mass, the priest prepares the bread and
wine for the sacrament of Eucharist. He prays:

On the night before he died for us,
he had supper for the last time with his friends.
He took bread
and gave thanks to God his Father.
He broke the bread
and gave it to his friends, saying:
Take this, all of you, and eat it:
this is my body which will be
   given up for you.
In the same way he took a cup of wine.
He gave thanks to God
and handed the cup
   to his friends, saying:
Take this, all of you,
   and drink from it:
this is the cup of my blood,
the blood of the new and
   unending promise.
It will be shed for you
   and for all
so that sins may be forgiven.
Then he said to them:
do this in memory of me.

Based on Eucharistic Prayer for
Masses with Children III

The Meal of God's People

The Mass is both a sacrifice and a celebration. During the **Liturgy of the Eucharist**, we remember the Last Supper. We also remember the death and Resurrection of Jesus Christ.

The Mass is also a holy meal for God's People today. In the **Eucharist**, the Holy Spirit changes the bread and wine into the Body and Blood of Jesus Christ.

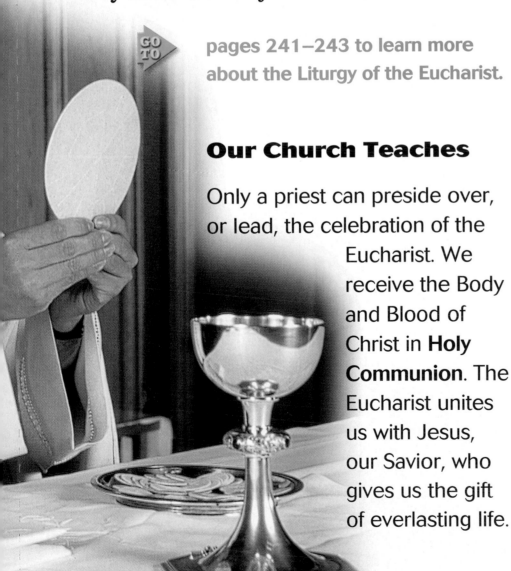

GO TO pages 241–243 to learn more about the Liturgy of the Eucharist.

Our Church Teaches

Only a priest can preside over, or lead, the celebration of the Eucharist. We receive the Body and Blood of Christ in **Holy Communion**. The Eucharist unites us with Jesus, our Savior, who gives us the gift of everlasting life.

We Believe

Christ is truly present in the bread and wine at Mass. In them, Christ gives us himself, the Bread of Life.

Faith Words

Eucharist
The Eucharist is a sacrifice and a special meal of thanks. In the Eucharist, God gives us the Body and Blood of Christ.

How do church members receive communion?

Going to Communion

Mr. Wills was teaching religion to a group of girls and boys. He said, "Tell me what you know about receiving communion."

Up shot every hand in the group!

Paolo answered first. "I must have already received Reconciliation before my First Communion," he said.

Mike added, "I must be free of serious sin."

Lucy said, "I shouldn't eat or drink anything but water for one hour before receiving communion."

April added, "I can receive communion either in the hand or on the tongue."

"And when the priest or the eucharistic minister says **the Body of Christ**, I should answer **Amen**," said Buddy.

Kye said, "I also say Amen when I hear **the Blood of Christ** if I receive from the cup, or chalice."

Then Ken said softly, "After communion, I return to my seat. I give thanks, because I have received the gift of Eucharist."

"Wow!" said Mr. Wills. "You didn't forget a thing!"

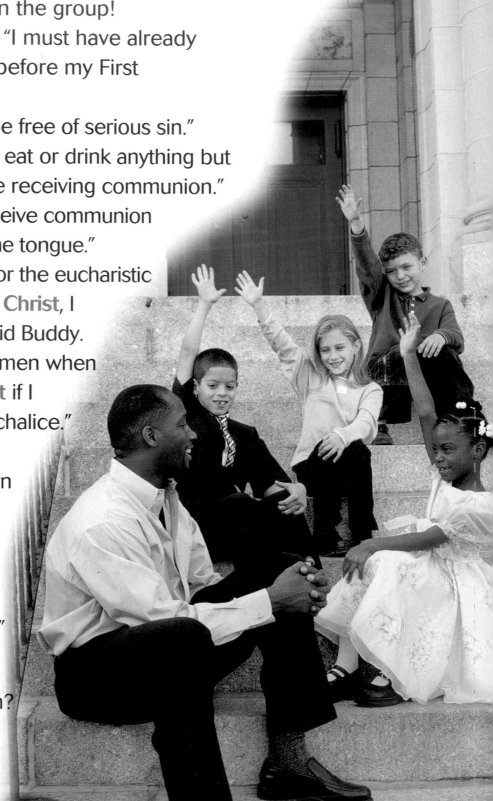

? What do you do after receiving communion?

Activity

Where you see a **Q**, an **X**, or a **Z** in the puzzle, cross it out.

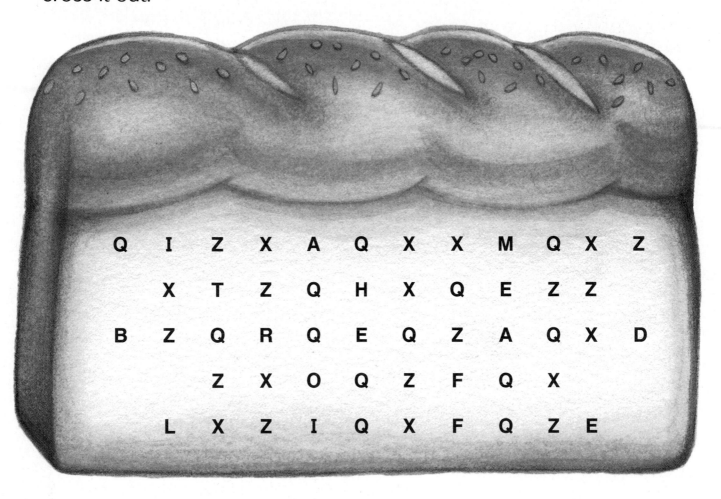

Q I Z X A Q X X M Q X Z

X T Z Q H X Q E Z Z

B Z Q R Q E Q Z A Q X D

Z X O Q Z F Q X

L X Z I Q X F Q Z E

Write the sentence you found in the puzzle.

_____

- -

_____

_____

- -

_____

- -

_____ .

How can we celebrate being one with Jesus?

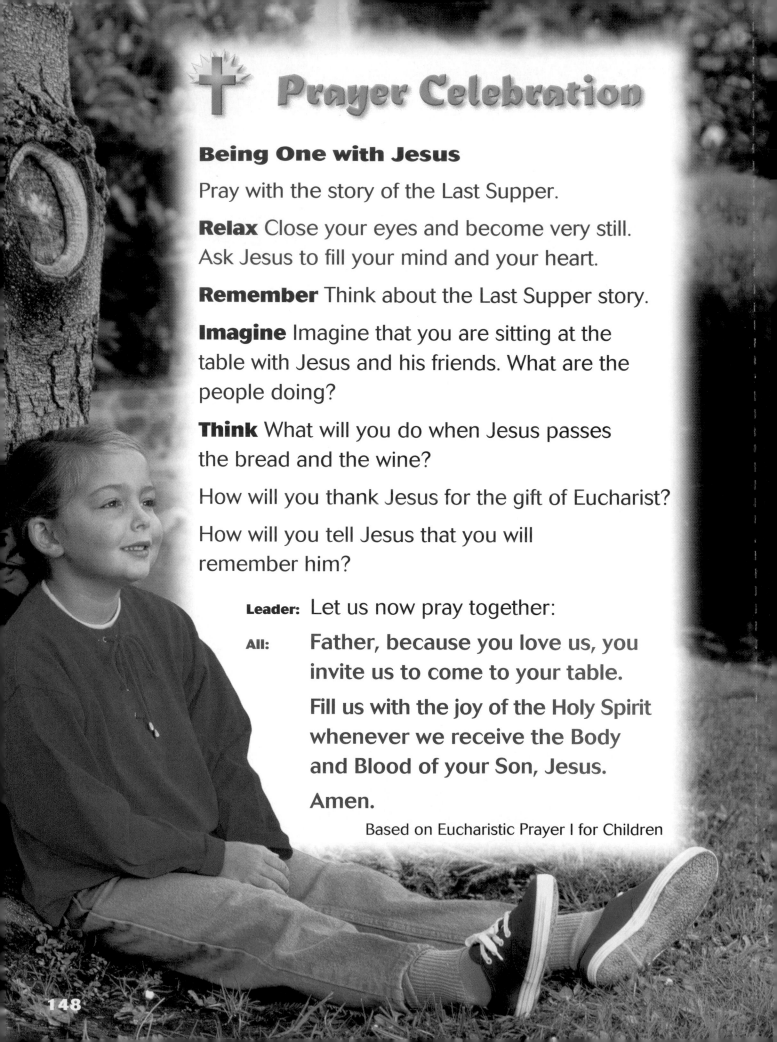

✝ Prayer Celebration

Being One with Jesus

Pray with the story of the Last Supper.

Relax Close your eyes and become very still. Ask Jesus to fill your mind and your heart.

Remember Think about the Last Supper story.

Imagine Imagine that you are sitting at the table with Jesus and his friends. What are the people doing?

Think What will you do when Jesus passes the bread and the wine?

How will you thank Jesus for the gift of Eucharist?

How will you tell Jesus that you will remember him?

Leader: Let us now pray together:

All: Father, because you love us, you invite us to come to your table.

Fill us with the joy of the Holy Spirit whenever we receive the Body and Blood of your Son, Jesus.

Amen.

Based on Eucharistic Prayer I for Children

FAMILY TIME

A choice of things to do at home

We Carry On the Work of Jesus

Chapter 15 presents the New Commandment that Jesus gave us about loving one another. Children will discover how Jesus showed his love for people. They will also identify ways that they can show their love for others.

What matters most?

We carry on the work of Jesus by knowing what our priorities are. With your family, talk about priorities. To explain the meaning of *priority*, use phrases such as *most important* and *do first things first*. Then have a quiz game. Ask each other "Which is most important. . ." questions, such as ". . .watching a video, writing a thank-you note, or filling the ice-cube trays?"

Choose one

With your child's help, think of different tasks any family member could do, such as putting away toys or folding towels. Together, write the tasks on slips of paper, fold them, and place them in a bowl. Then have each person take one slip from the bowl each day and complete the task.

Have a heart

With your child, make a large red paper heart and put it on display. Keep a box of adhesive bandage strips nearby. Have your child put one on the heart whenever any family member does an act of healing to make someone feel better.

✝ A Prayer for the Week

Through your works,
Lord, you showed your love.
Help us carry on your work
with acts of kindness,
healing, and love.
Amen.

FAMILY TIME

Something to Do . . .

On Sunday

As you pray silently during the prayer after communion, reflect on how you will love others as Jesus loves you.

Through the Week

To show love for their family, members can make an effort to lend a hand with indoor and outdoor tasks.

Visit Our Web Site

 www.blestarewe.com

Something to Think About . . .

The Example of Jesus

My daughter is at the point of death. Please, come lay your hands on her that she may get well and live.

Mark 5:23

 In the Gospel story about Jairus and his daughter, Jesus heals a girl who relatives and friends think is dead. When he takes the girl's hand and tells her to get up, she rises immediately. Through the healing power of Jesus, she is completely well, to the utter astonishment of her family.

This is a striking account of the way Jesus showed his love for everyone, setting an example for us to love others.

Something to Know About . . .

Our Heritage in Holy People

Damien de Veuster is a holy person who risked his life as he cared for others. Born in Belgium in 1840, as a young man he entered the Congregation of the Sacred Hearts. He volunteered to serve in the Hawaiian missions. Father Damien spent eight years in the missions, carrying on the work of Jesus.

In 1866 a sickness called Hansen's disease, better known as leprosy, spread across the Hawaiian Islands. The lepers were exiled to the island of Molokai. Father Damien volunteered to care for them. He kept their bodies and their bandages clean; he built houses

and coffins; he practiced untold works of charity. Father Damien contracted the disease himself in 1876, dying of leprosy in 1889.

This holy man represents Hawaii in Statuary Hall in Washington, D.C. On June 4, 1995, Damien de Veuster was beatified by Pope John Paul II.

15 We Carry On the Work of Jesus

 Love one another as I have loved you.

Based on John 13:34

Share

What kind of workers do you see?

What kind of work would you like to do when you grow up? Show it in a drawing.

 What work did Jesus do?

Hear & Believe

Jesus and the Little Girl

Storyteller: Jesus was speaking to a crowd of people. A man named Jairus was there.

Jairus: (kneels in front of Jesus) Lord, please come to my home and see my sick daughter.

Jesus: Show me the way. I will help her.

Jairus: (gets up) Thank you, Jesus. Let's go!

Storyteller: They started walking. Then a servant girl ran up to them.

Servant: Sir, your daughter just died.

Storyteller: Jairus was very sad.

Jesus: Do not be afraid, Jairus. I can still help.

Storyteller: When they got to the house, Jesus went in. The dead girl was lying on the bed.

Jesus: (holding her hand) Little girl, get up!

Storyteller: The little girl got up at once. She ran to hug her father.

Jairus: Jesus, how can I ever thank you?

Jesus: Try to love everyone as I have loved you.

Based on Mark 5:21–24, 35–42

The Work of Jesus

Jesus showed his love for Jairus and his daughter. Jesus always loved everyone. Jesus also taught people about God's love for them. He did this in many ways. He told stories. He shared food. He forgave sinners. He comforted people who were sad. Jesus healed the sick. He even brought dead people back to life.

Our Church Teaches

In the **New Commandment** Jesus said, "Love one another as I have loved you." This is the law of love. We are called to love others the way God loves us. We live by Jesus' law of love when we show our love for others.

What are some ordinary ways we can love others?

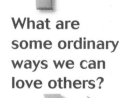

153

Taking Care of Others

"Mrs. Nye wasn't at Mass today," said Mattie. "She was at home, sick and alone. She couldn't even cook!

"Everybody wanted to help. Dr. Ray stopped in to see Mrs. Nye. Joey Garcia brought her a nice lunch. He stayed and visited for a while. The Grant family prepared her dinner."

"So that took care of Sunday. What about the rest of the week?" asked Kim.

"We'll deliver Mrs. Nye's meals every day. Many people will visit her. And I will ask everybody in the parish to pray for Mrs. Nye.

"You know, Jesus taught us to love one another as he loved us. When we take care of Mrs. Nye, we show our love for God!"

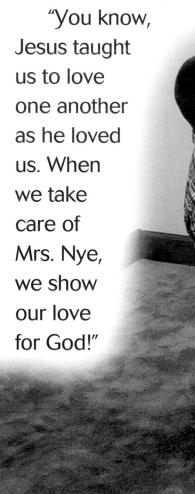

Activities

Show how you can carry on the work of Jesus.

1. Write four words you can say to someone who is sad.

   _____   _____

   _____   _____

   _____   _____

2. Draw a picture that shows how you can help a sick person.

How can we pray a simple prayer for others?

Prayer Celebration

The Thumb Prayer

You can pray for others by using just your thumb. Trace a small Sign of the Cross with your thumb. On the downward stroke of the cross, whisper "Jesus." On the sideways stroke, whisper the name of someone you are praying for. You might whisper "Jesus," then "Uncle Tim." You can trace the thumb cross anywhere—in the palm of your hand, on a book, on your pillow at night, or on the seat of a car.

Choose one of the thumb prayers below. Decide where you will make your crosses. Then say your prayer over and over again.

Jesus, the Pope.
Jesus, all parents.
Jesus, those in need.
Jesus, Father Doyle.
Jesus, all children.
Jesus, (your own prayer).

FAMILY TIME

A choice of things to do at home

We Pray Like Jesus

We call God "our Father" because Jesus asked us to, and we pray the Lord's Prayer because Jesus taught it to us. In Chapter 16, children learn to pray the Lord's Prayer with an understanding of its meaning. The children will also identify the parts of the day in which they might pray.

Daily bread

The bread that we eat every day may be very different from the bread Jesus ate, or from the breads eaten in other parts of the world. Serve a variety of breads this week (raisin, pita, sourdough, French, Italian, cornbread). Talk about how daily bread is needed by everyone.

Making conversation

Some conversations focus on asking for things, while others focus on solving problems. Still others focus on praising or apologizing. With your child, list several purposes of conversation. Remind your child that when we pray, we talk to and listen to God.

Pray all ways

Discuss with your child different ways you can pray, such as by singing, by using gestures, by meditating, by praying words you have learned by heart, or by using your own words. Practice using some of these prayer forms together.

> ✝ **A Prayer for the Week**
>
> Jesus, thank you for teaching us the Lord's Prayer. It reminds us that we can ask God our Father for what we need. Help us always pray it with an open heart.
> Amen.

FAMILY TIME

Something to Do...

On Sunday

Say a prayer of gratitude for the life-affirming bread of the Eucharist.

Through the Week

Each day this week, say a family prayer at a different time. Some suggested times are bedtime, mealtime, before leaving home in the morning, or before doing homework.

Visit Our Web Site

 www.blestarewe.com

Something to Think About...

The Essence of Prayer

This is how you are to pray:
Our Father in heaven,
hallowed be your name.
Matthew 6:9

Jesus taught the Lord's Prayer to his followers when they asked him how they should pray. The Lord's Prayer is so important that we pray it at every Mass; it summarizes the whole Gospel of God's love. In a concise series of statements, Jesus taught us how to pray. He praised God and asked for food, forgiveness, and to be kept from temptation. Through the years we have repeated this prayer, regarding it as the very essence of prayer. As we teach the Lord's Prayer to our children, we share our recognition of its value, its beauty, and its centrality to Christian life.

Something to Know About...

Our Heritage in Symbols

In Jesus' time, people sometimes used objects as they prayed. Palm branches were used during prayers of praise. The waving branches symbolized victory. Jesus' followers held palm branches during his triumphant entry into Jerusalem before his passion and death.

Traditionally, palms are blessed at the beginning of the liturgy on Palm Sunday. The ashes that are crossed on our foreheads on Ash Wednesday come from burned palms. Some families place palms behind a hanging crucifix or holy picture. Other traditions include braiding palms into crosses or burning them slightly when there is a bad storm or some other such crisis.

16 We Pray Like Jesus

Let us call to the Lord at all times.
Let us praise God both day and night.

Based on Psalm 34:2

Share

Many people do things at the same time each day.

At 7:00 A.M., Betsy wakes up.
What time do you usually wake up?

_____

_____

At 8:00 A.M., Willie gets on the bus.
What time do you go to school?

_____

_____

At 6:00 P.M., the Diaz family eats dinner.
What time does your family eat dinner?

_____

_____

Talk about what time things happen on Saturday.

Tell what is different about Sunday.

How did Jesus pray?

159

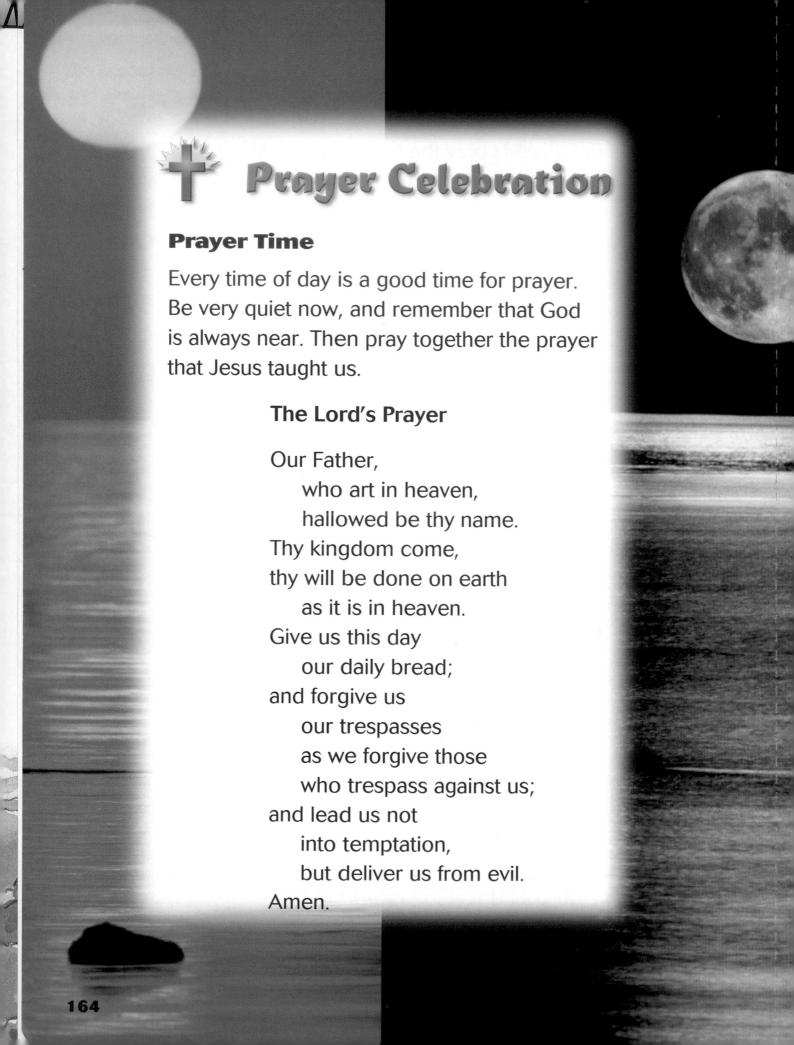

✝ Prayer Celebration

Prayer Time

Every time of day is a good time for prayer. Be very quiet now, and remember that God is always near. Then pray together the prayer that Jesus taught us.

The Lord's Prayer

Our Father,
who art in heaven,
hallowed be thy name.
Thy kingdom come,
thy will be done on earth
as it is in heaven.
Give us this day
our daily bread;
and forgive us
our trespasses
as we forgive those
who trespass against us;
and lead us not
into temptation,
but deliver us from evil.
Amen.

WE CARE About Parish and Community

Caring and Sharing

The children in the parish that Taylor belongs to did something really neat. They brought some of their used books to the Parish Hall. Their religion teacher had told them about some poor children in town. These boys and girls had no money to buy picture books, or storybooks, or comic books. The parish gave the used books to the poor children.

Many boys and girls gave away their old books. Some books were about sports. Others were about famous people. Others told exciting stories. The boys and girls thought about how much they had enjoyed reading them! They hoped that the poor children would like them that much, too!

Do you have anything you could share with poor children?

Think About It

Suppose that you have never had a book to read and enjoy. Imagine what that would be like! It's hard to believe, but some poor children have no books at all!

Write the name of your favorite book.

Learn About It

Jesus said, "Love one another as I have loved you." He teaches us to treat everyone fairly and to help poor people. That is what the children did in the story on page 165.

Do Something About It

Do you have books or other things that you could give away? Think of things like clothes and sneakers that don't fit you anymore. Do you have toys, a bike, or video games that you don't use?

Write words that name extra things you could share with poor children.

Use the chapter titles to complete the sentences.

Jesus saves us from
_____
- - - - - - - - - - - - - - - - - - - -
_____.

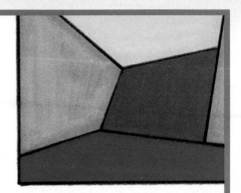

We carry on the
_____
- - - - - - - - - - - - - - - - - - - -
_____
of Jesus.

We receive the gift
_____
- - - - - - - - - - - - - - - - - - - -
of _____.

_____
- - - - - - - - - - - - - - - - - - - -
We _____
like Jesus.

A Remember the story "Jesus Gives Up His Life."
Write 1, 2, and 3 in the boxes to put the
story in order.

☐ An angel said that Jesus was raised from the dead.

☐ Soldiers nailed Jesus to a wooden cross.

☐ After Jesus died, his friends buried him.

B Draw a line to the word that completes
each sentence.

1. God's greatest gift to us is   ●   ● Savior

2. Jesus gave his life as a sacrifice
   for our   ●   ● Jesus

3. Jesus' rising from the dead is
   called the   ●   ● sins

4. Sometimes we call Jesus our   ●   ● Resurrection

C Draw a line under each sentence that tells
about Saint Elizabeth of Hungary.

She kept her jewels.

She helped the poor.

She loved Jesus.

She was selfish.

D Write the correct word to complete each sentence.

1. The _____ is a sacrifice and a celebration.
   Church   Bible   Mass

2. During the Liturgy of the Eucharist we remember the _____.
   Bread   Last Supper   First People

3. _____ is truly present in the blessed bread and wine at Mass.
   Peter   Christ   John

4. At Holy Communion, Jesus Christ gives us _____ in the bread and wine.
   himself   Mary   families

E Read the sentences below. In the heart, write the word that completes every sentence.

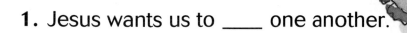

1. Jesus wants us to ____ one another.

2. Jesus gave us the law of ____.

3. By loving others, we show ____ for God.

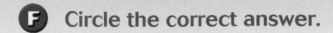

UNIT 4 Review

F Circle the correct answer.

1. Jesus taught us how to pray the ____.
   temptation   Lord's Prayer   bread

2. Hallowed means ____.
   bread   perfect   holy

3. Sins or wrongs we do on purpose are ____.
   trespasses   Lord's Prayer   grace

4. Wanting to do something wrong is called ____.
   blessed   temptation   hallowed

5. We pray for our daily ____.
   evil   kingdom   bread

6. We ask God to deliver us from ____.
   evil   goodness   prayer

G Write two words to complete the banner.

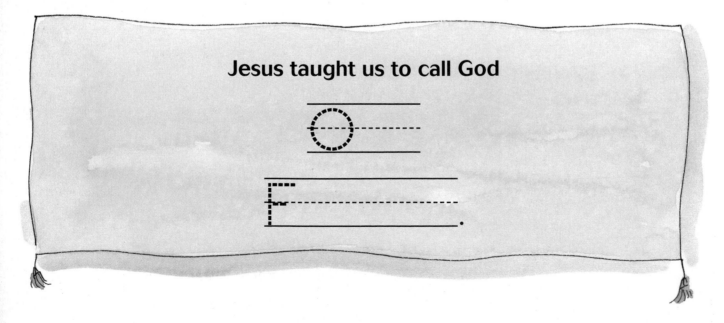

Jesus taught us to call God

_____
O_____

_____
F_____.

We Go in Peace

Made stronger by the Eucharist, we work to be more like Christ in all we do. We can help others know about Jesus by the way we treat them.

Blessed are the peacemakers,
for they will be called
children of God.

Matthew 5:9

Christ's first disciples may have walked this street in Jerusalem spreading a message of peace. At the end of Mass we also go in peace to serve all people.

Alleluia

Music by Fintan O'Carroll

Al - le - lu - ia, al - le - lu - ia!

Al - le - lu - ia, al - le - lu - ia!

FAMILY TIME

A choice of things to do at home

God Gives Us the Holy Spirit

God gives us the Holy Spirit to guide us in our daily lives. The children will come to understand that the Holy Spirit is our helper, guide, and teacher. They will think about and appreciate the spiritual gifts that Paul writes about in the Scripture passage.

Matching gifts

Have a gift night! Each person can give a small present to one other family member. Choose names beforehand so that everyone gets a present. The present should represent a gift the person has. For example, if someone draws well, the gift might be a sketch pad.

Wisdom

A wise person considers things from different points of view and thinks about the outcome of the things he or she says. With your child, make a list of people you consider wise—in your family, in school, in your community, or in the news.

We are gifted

Talk with your child about some qualities you and other adults in your family may have, such as kindness and helpfulness. Explain that these are gifts that God has given and that people have developed. Then discuss with your child which of God's gifts he or she can develop.

✝ A Prayer for the Week
Holy Spirit, thank you for the gifts of wisdom and knowledge. Your gifts help us be faithful followers of Jesus. Amen.

FAMILY TIME

Something to Do . . .

On Sunday

Pray for the people who, in the name of the congregation, bring the gifts in the offertory procession.

Through the Week

In many cultures, the elders of the community are considered especially wise. Talk to or visit an elderly relative or neighbor this week.

Visit Our Web Site

 www.blestarewe.com

Something to Think About . . .

Different Gifts

There are different kinds of spiritual gifts but the same Spirit; there are different forms of service but the same Lord; there are different workings but the same God who produces all of them in everyone.
1 Corinthians 12:4–6

Saint Paul explains what spiritual gifts are and how they are distributed. Some of the gifts that he discusses include the gifts of wisdom, knowledge, faith, and healing. He says that one Spirit produces all of these gifts, which are distributed individually to each person. We all have different functions in the community and therefore receive different gifts. In our family, the same is true. People have different functions in the family and therefore need different gifts. It's not up to us to decide which gifts we think people should have. We should be thankful for the gifts we have, and we should use them to help others.

Something to Know About . . . Our Heritage in Architecture

The Hagia Sofia, Greek for "holy wisdom," was built in the sixth century by the emperor Justinian I in Constantinople, now Istanbul, Turkey. The cathedral was named for the gift of the Holy Spirit and remains one of the finest examples of Byzantine architecture. After the Turks conquered Constantinople in the fifteenth century, the Hagia Sophia became a mosque, or Islamic house of worship. Its mosaics and Christian symbols were covered with plaster. The Hagia Sofia stayed that way until the twentieth century, when it became a museum and some of its original mosaics were uncovered.

17 God Gives Us the Holy Spirit

 God has sent the Holy Spirit into our hearts.

Based on Galatians 4:6

Share

All people have special gifts. These gifts are part of who we are. We can use these gifts to help others.

Some people are smart. They can help others learn.

Some people are funny. They can cheer up people who are sad.

Some people are kind and helpful. They can make life easier for others.

What is one special gift you have?

_____

I can _____.

How can you use this gift to help others?

What are spiritual gifts?

The Special Gifts

Paul had friends who lived in the city of Corinth. These friends asked Paul about the best way to serve God and their community. Paul wrote them this letter.

Dear Friends,

God loves you very much. He sent the Holy Spirit to help you live as good followers of Jesus.

One way the Holy Spirit helps is by giving special gifts to each person. These special gifts are called **spiritual gifts**. Some of these gifts are wisdom, healing, knowledge, and faith. The Holy Spirit may give one person the gift of wisdom. He may give another person the gift of healing. To someone else, he may give knowledge or faith.

God wants you to show your love for him by sharing your gifts with each other and with the Church. Remember, the Church needs each person's gifts!

Peace and love,
Paul

Based on 1 Corinthians 12:4–11

Gifts to Share

Paul wrote in his letter that the Holy Spirit gives each of us special, spiritual gifts. Some examples are knowledge, wisdom, healing, and faith. We show our love for God by using our gifts to help others.

Our Church Teaches

The Holy Spirit is our helper, guide, and teacher. He leads us in our daily lives. The Holy Spirit helps us share our spiritual gifts with other people and with the Church.

What can we do with the gifts we have been given?

177

Respond
Using Our Gifts

Religion class had just started. Mrs. Foy asked, "How do you use your spiritual gifts to help others?"

Gino said, "I help my little sister learn to count. That's how I use my gift of knowledge."

"Sometimes Dad gets hot and tired from working outdoors. I bring him a nice cold drink. That's how I use my gift of healing," added Tara.

Kathy said "I use the gift of wisdom when I make good choices."

"All of us use the gift of faith when we trust in God," said Jake.

? How do you use your spiritual gifts to help others?

Activities

1. Sometimes we use symbols to stand for the Holy Spirit. Some symbols are a white dove, wind, flames, and rays of light. Color the symbols and the words in the banner.

2. God wants us to open our hearts to the Holy Spirit. God wants us to use the gifts we have been given.

Put a ✓ under **Yes** if the person is using his or her gifts. Put a ✓ under **No** if the person is not using his or her gifts.

	Yes	No
a. Janet receives a letter from Grandma. She does not answer it.	☐	☐
b. Carlos shares his popcorn with Miguel and Ricardo.	☐	☐
c. Mike can read. He does not want to help his little sister learn to read.	☐	☐
d. Debra can draw beautiful pictures. She draws one for Aunt Sue.	☐	☐
e. Susan likes to sing. She sings in the children's choir at Mass.	☐	☐
f. Robert plays the piano very well, but he will not play for others.	☐	☐
g. Tanya tells bedtime stories to her little sister.	☐	☐

How can we celebrate our spiritual gifts?

Prayer Celebration

We Pray to the Holy Spirit

The Holy Spirit helps us pray. Here is a prayer you can pray to the Holy Spirit.

Leader: We have been given gifts by the Holy Spirit. Close your eyes now, and think about a special gift that you have. (pause)

Leader: Let us pray that we may always use our gifts to help others.

Side 1: Breathe in me, O Holy Spirit,

Side 2: That my thoughts may be holy;

Side 1: Act in me, O Holy Spirit,

Side 2: That my work may be holy;

Side 1: Fill my heart, O Holy Spirit,

Side 2: That I love only what is holy;

Side 1: Strengthen me, O Holy Spirit,

Side 2: To defend all that is holy;

Side 1: Guard me, O Holy Spirit,

Side 2: That I always may be holy.

Based on the Holy Spirit Prayer of St. Augustine

FAMILY TIME

A choice of things to do at home

We Celebrate Peace and Service

The children will learn that we greet each other at Mass by offering those around us a Sign of Peace. This sign reminds us that Jesus wants us to get along with everyone and to serve one another.

Greetings

Play a game with your child in which you take turns making different gestures to say Hello, such as waving. Be creative and see how many turns you can take without repeating the same gesture.

Switch with me

To better understand how each person serves the family, switch chores and responsibilities in the family. At the end of the week, change again, so that everyone has a chance to serve in different ways.

Called to service

Talk with your child about different people who work in your church. Ask your child to think of as many people as possible. Explain how these people are actively serving in the life of your parish.

✝ A Prayer for the Week

Welcome us to your table, Lord. Help us see your presence in everyone we know. Help us be people who share and serve. Amen.

FAMILY TIME

Something to Do ...

On Sunday

Remind each other to think about making peace in the family as you share the Sign of Peace at Mass.

Through the Week

Talk with your family about the importance of getting along with everyone and serving one another in your family and parish.

Visit Our Web Site

 www.blestarewe.com

Something to Know About ...

Our Heritage in Religious Life

Blessed Jeanne Jugan, Marie of the Cross (1792–1879), grew up as a poor French girl. From her youth she felt that she was called to do something special. In 1837, with another woman and a teenage orphan girl, she formed a community of prayer and good works. From that small beginning, she established an order called the Little Sisters of the Poor, whose mission is to care for the needy elderly. In addition to the vows of poverty, chastity, and obedience, this group takes a vow of hospitality. On October 3, 1982, Jeanne Jugan was beatified by Pope John Paul II. Today, there are Little Sisters of the Poor in thirty countries, on five continents.

Something to Think About ...

Cooperating in Service

The peace of the Lord be with you always.
The Order of Mass

The Sign of Peace is a sign of the Holy Spirit, a greeting, and a reminder that we should get along with everyone. The Sign of Peace is also a reminder that we are to serve others. Belonging to the Catholic Church is not like membership in a club. It is more like being part of a cooperative endeavor, where everyone has a job to do. Because everyone cooperates, the Church is able to accomplish things it otherwise would have neither the money nor the personnel to do. Because some church members conduct worship, others raise families, and still others take on church-related jobs of education and service, the community runs smoothly. On Sunday we come together to celebrate our unity.

18 We Celebrate Peace and Service

Greet one another with a sign of peace.

Based on 2 Corinthians 13:11

Share

We greet other people with words or with actions.
How can you greet someone without using words?

The people in the pictures want to say "Hello."
But each of them wants to say it in a different way.
Write a different greeting in each person's balloon.

How do
we greet
each other
at Mass?

Hear & Believe

The Sign of Peace

At each Eucharist, we offer those around us a Sign of Peace. Peace is a sign that the Holy Spirit is with us. The Sign of Peace reminds us that Jesus wants us to get along with everyone. It also reminds us that we are to serve one another each day.

Here is the Sign of Peace you take part in during Mass.

Priest: Lord Jesus Christ, you said to your apostles:
I leave you peace, my peace I give you.
Look not on our sins, but on the faith of your Church,
and grant us the peace and unity of your kingdom
where you live for ever and ever.

All: Amen.

Priest: The peace of the Lord be with you always.

All: And also with you.

Priest: Let us offer each other the sign of peace.

The Order of Mass

We Take Part and Serve

The Sign of Peace reminds us that Jesus wants us to love one another and to have peace. It calls all members of the Church to serve one another. The Sign of Peace reminds us to take part in parish activities.

Our Church Teaches

Men who become deacons, priests, and bishops receive the sacrament of **Holy Orders**. They lead the Church community in celebrating the sacraments and teaching the Gospel.

Baptized men and women receive the sacrament of **Matrimony** from each other. They promise to be faithful to each other for their whole lives. They serve the Church by caring for their families and sharing in the work of their parish.

We Believe

Holy Orders and Matrimony are sacraments of service. All members of the Church are called to live in peace and serve others.

Faith Words

Holy Orders
Holy Orders is a sacrament of service.

Matrimony
Matrimony is a sacrament of service.

How can we celebrate our call to service?

Hearing the Call

Karol Wojtyla (say "voy TEE wah") was a boy who grew up in a town in Poland. When he was a baby, he heard church bells ringing every day. He didn't know it yet, but the bells were calling the people to pray.

Karol loved to be outdoors and he loved sports. His friends called him to play soccer. Bright sunshine called him to take a boat ride. The forests called him to go hiking. The mountains called him to ski.

On November 1, 1946, Karol celebrated the sacrament of Holy Orders. God had called Karol to spend his life in the service of the Church. First he was a priest, then a bishop, then a cardinal. Karol's name is now John Paul II. He was called to be the pope!

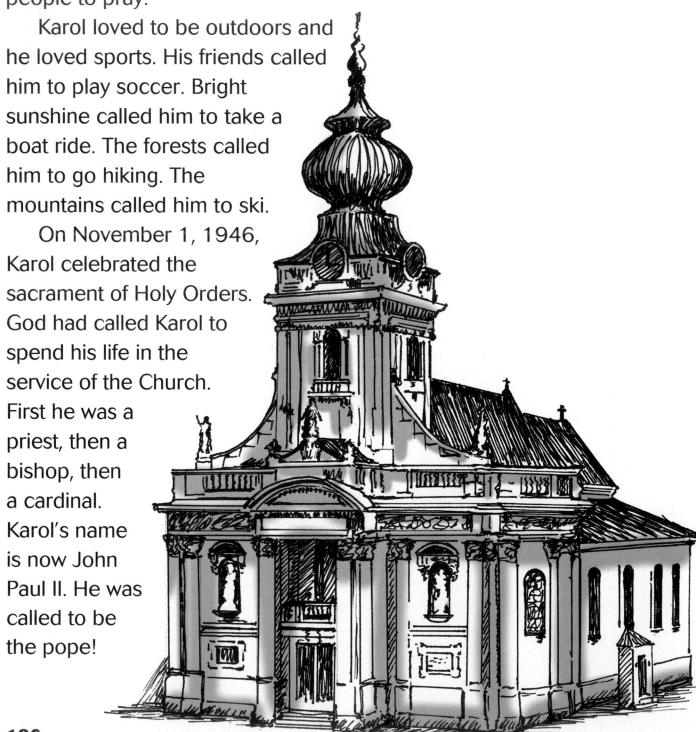

Activities

1. Find the hidden message. Write it on the line below the picture. Then color the picture.

_____

_____ .

2. Complete these sentences.

A bride and groom celebrate the sacrament of

_____

_____ .

When a man becomes a priest, he receives

_____

_____ .

How can we celebrate people who serve others?

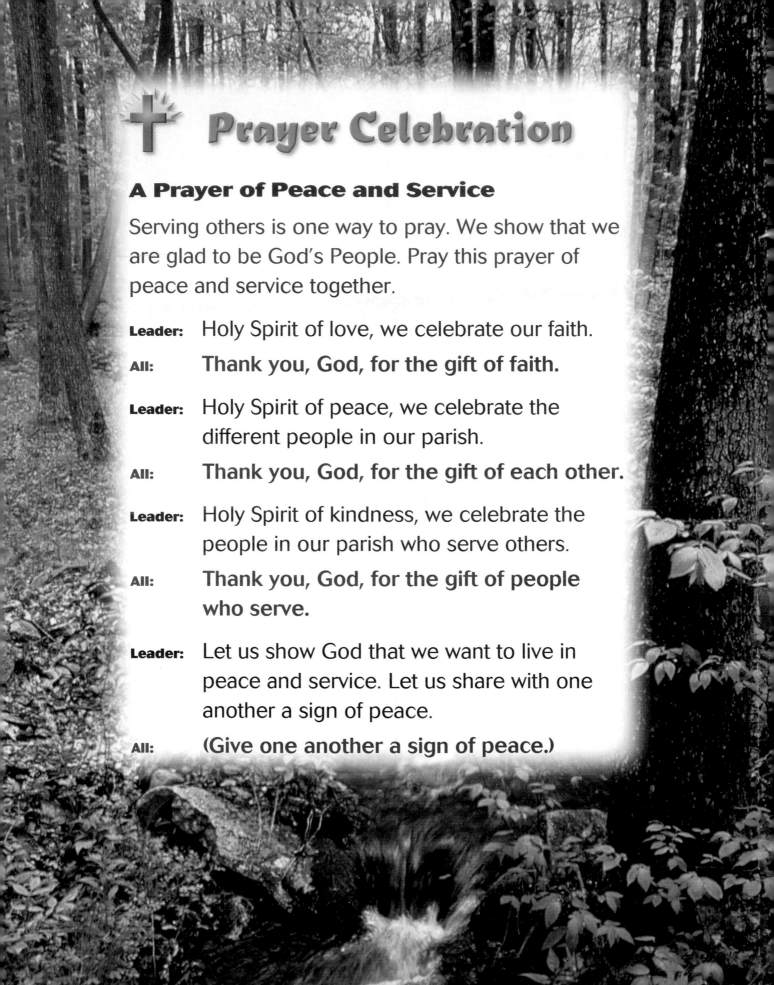

✝ Prayer Celebration

A Prayer of Peace and Service

Serving others is one way to pray. We show that we are glad to be God's People. Pray this prayer of peace and service together.

Leader: Holy Spirit of love, we celebrate our faith.

All: **Thank you, God, for the gift of faith.**

Leader: Holy Spirit of peace, we celebrate the different people in our parish.

All: **Thank you, God, for the gift of each other.**

Leader: Holy Spirit of kindness, we celebrate the people in our parish who serve others.

All: **Thank you, God, for the gift of people who serve.**

Leader: Let us show God that we want to live in peace and service. Let us share with one another a sign of peace.

All: **(Give one another a sign of peace.)**

FAMILY TIME

A choice of things to do at home

We Work for Peace and Justice

The saying "If you want peace, work for justice" sums up the Christian belief in the interconnectedness of the two. We are called to treat others fairly and with respect. In Chapter 19 children will consider the concepts of peace and justice and identify actions they can take to promote these concepts. The children will realize that Jesus taught us to treat others fairly and respectfully.

Certificate of fairness

With your child, make a simple certificate with construction paper and bright-colored decorations. Help your child write the words *Fairness Counts* at the top. List words associated with fairness, such as *sharing*, *helping*, and *giving*. Each time your child acts fairly this week, give her or him a sticker to add to the certificate.

Peace party

With your child, plan a family peace party. Instead of the Nobel peace prize, give a prize named after your family. Tell what the winner did to earn the prize. Pencils with peace signs on them or chocolate coins make good prizes.

Just desserts

The phrase "get one's just deserts" means "get a fair reward or punishment." But the sound-alike word *desserts* also presents a good way to learn about fairness. Try using a system in which one person cuts a piece of dessert in two, and another person chooses which piece to take.

A Prayer for the Week

In your eyes we are all equal, Lord. You have made all of us in your image. Help us learn, in your name, to love everyone equally.
Amen.

FAMILY TIME

Something to Do . . .

On Sunday

Other than in the Sign of Peace, when is peace mentioned in the liturgy? Listen for other mentions of peace.

Through the Week

Find peaceful, fair ways to resolve differences that arise in your family. Encourage family members to respect one another.

Visit Our Web Site

 www.blestarewe.com

Something to Think About . . .

Sharing Earthly Goods

The community of believers was of one heart and mind, and no one claimed that any of his possessions was his own, but they had everything in common.
Acts 4:32

The early Christians followed Jesus' teachings of peace and justice by making things fair for everyone and by treating others as they wanted to be treated themselves. The sharing of earthly goods was characteristic of the early Christians. They were able to claim that there was no one in their community who went without what they needed to live.

We are challenged to share our goods cheerfully, out of love for the Lord. As we work toward the goal of meeting everyone's needs, we are spreading the Gospel because we are sharing with people who have less than they need. When we do what is right, God's Spirit is with us.

Something to Know About . . . Our Heritage in Art

Edward Hicks was a Pennsylvania Quaker minister, a carriage maker, a sign and furniture painter, and an artist. He lived in the late eighteenth– and early–nineteenth centuries. Hicks became one of the best–known American folk artists. He painted more than one hundred versions of *The Peaceable Kingdom*, based on the prophecy of Isaiah 11:6-9. Isaiah prophesied that in God's peaceable kingdom, the wolf would lie down with the lamb and a little child would lead all creatures. Hicks painted wild animals and children existing in peace together. Because Jesus was born as a human baby, some people thought that Jesus fulfilled Isaiah's prophecy.

19 We Work for Peace and Justice

Happy are those who are fair with others.
Happy are those who make peace.

Based on Matthew 5:6, 9

Share

Life is not always fair. Some people are rich, while others are poor. Some people are healthy, while others are sick.

Look at the pictures. Use a ✔ to mark each one **fair** or **unfair**.

She shares.

☐ fair   ☐ unfair

He steals.

☐ fair   ☐ unfair

She helps.

☐ fair   ☐ unfair

He gives.

☐ fair   ☐ unfair

She peeks.

☐ fair   ☐ unfair

How does Jesus want us to act?

191

✝ The First Followers of Jesus

The first followers of Jesus tried to be fair to everyone. If life was not fair, they tried to help make it more fair. Here is how the early Christians treated one another.

The Christians were all of one heart and
    one mind.
They tried to make peace and they tried to
    be kind.
They shared what they had, both the rich and
    the poor,
So no one went hungry or wanted for more.
Those who had extra would sell what they had
To take care of those who were sick or were sad.
If someone was needy, the church members came
With food and with money in Christ Jesus' name.

Based on Acts 4:32–35

What Jesus Taught

Jesus taught us to live in **peace**. When there is fighting, Christians try to make peace. Jesus also taught us to treat everyone with **justice**. We help people who need extra help. We share with people who have less.

Our Church Teaches

We should treat people the way we want others to treat us. We grow in holiness when we make peace and treat others fairly. We follow Jesus and grow closer to God.

Faith Words

peace
Peace means getting along with others.

justice
Justice means treating people as they deserve to be treated.

How can we make peace and act with justice?

Respond
Christian Peacemakers

Peacemakers try to make peace when there is fighting and trouble. They try to bring justice to people who need it. Here are some Christians who are peacemakers.

Doctor Johnson works with Operation Smile. He helps poor children by fixing their mouths so they can smile again.

Sammy helps keep peace in another country. He makes sure that fighting does not start again.

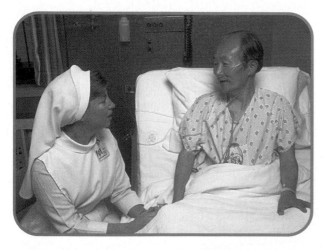

Sister Carole Martin helps people who are sick and dying. She shows them that God has not forgotten them.

Angela works in a shelter for women and children. She protects them from people who want to hurt them.

Activity

Get ready for the Prayer Celebration on page 196.
Learn to sign the words "Blessed are the peacemakers,
for they will be called children of God" (Matthew 5:9).

Blessed **peacemakers,**

they **will be** **called**

children **God**

How can we
celebrate
God's gifts of
peace and
justice?

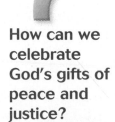

195

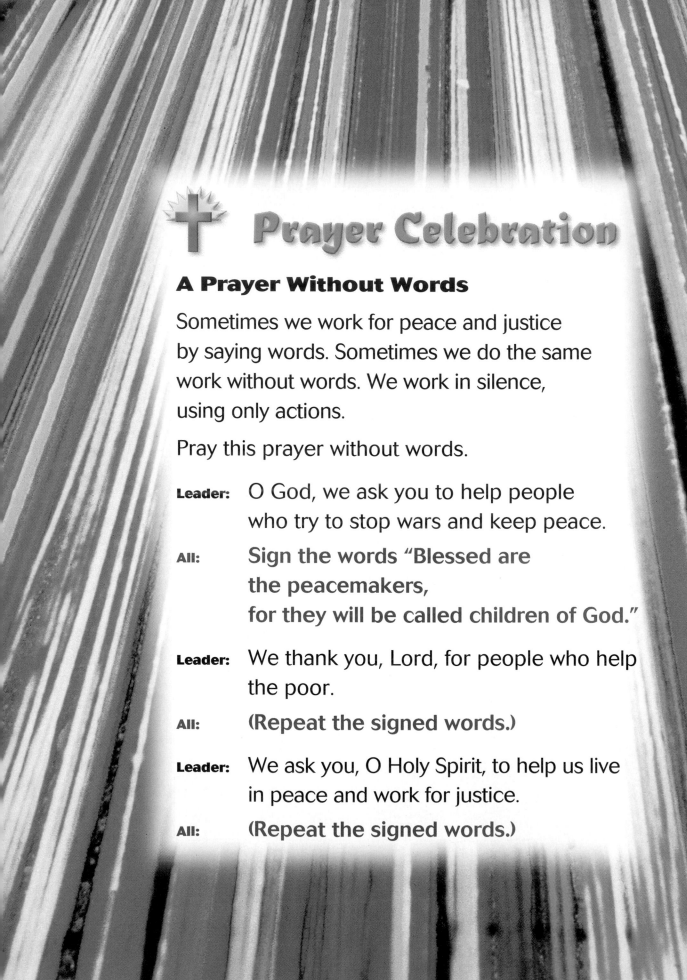

✝ Prayer Celebration

A Prayer Without Words

Sometimes we work for peace and justice by saying words. Sometimes we do the same work without words. We work in silence, using only actions.

Pray this prayer without words.

Leader: O God, we ask you to help people who try to stop wars and keep peace.

All: Sign the words "Blessed are the peacemakers, for they will be called children of God."

Leader: We thank you, Lord, for people who help the poor.

All: (Repeat the signed words.)

Leader: We ask you, O Holy Spirit, to help us live in peace and work for justice.

All: (Repeat the signed words.)

FAMILY TIME

A choice of things to do at home

We Go Forth in the Holy Spirit

Chapter 20 will highlight the virtue of peace and the beauty of blessings. Children will realize that blessings are signs of God's love, that we bless God when we praise and thank him, and that we can pray to God to bless others. They will recognize that the Holy Spirit guides us when we pray, and they will compose prayers of blessings.

Bedtime blessing

When your children go to bed this week, make a Sign of the Cross on each one's forehead and say, "Good night. God bless you." You will bring their day to a peaceful close.

Bless this mess

Some families have in their homes a sign that bears the motto "Bless this Mess." It invites God to be part of the family's life even though the house may not be perfectly neat and clean. With your child, make a sign that asks for God's blessing on the activities of your family.

Support peace

Some companies give a share of their profits to activities that promote peace and other good causes. Have your child help you look for a product your family would use made by a company that supports a good cause. Tell your family why you and your child selected the product.

✝ A Prayer for the Week

O God, thank you for the blessings you give us. Bless others as you have blessed us. Help us go forth in peace. Amen.

FAMILY TIME

Something to Do . . .

On Sunday

At the end of Mass when the priest says, "Go in peace to love and serve the Lord," think of one way to do that.

Through the Week

Think about the blessings you have, and take time to thank God. At dinner, take turns talking about your blessings.

Visit Our Web Site

 www.blestarewe.com

Something to Think About . . .

The Peace of the Lord

The LORD bless you and keep you!
The LORD look upon you kindly and give you peace!
Numbers 6:24, 26

 In the Scripture, God asks Moses to speak to his brother Aaron and to Aaron's sons to tell them how he wants them to bless others. God blesses us and gives us peace. In our lives we have moments when we experience real peace. We see the ocean or a sleeping child, and we have an experience that is free of worry, or plans, or anything but contentment. The peace of the Lord is like a continuation of that blessed moment. When we structure time in our home to allow for peace, we create an atmosphere for our family to receive the peace of Christ.

Something to Know About . . . Our Heritage in Architecture

In the place where Jesus spoke the Beatitudes to his followers, there is a church that is named after the famous blessings. The Church of the Beatitudes is located along the northern shore of the Sea of Galilee on the mount near Capernaum, home to five of Jesus' Twelve Apostles.

Built in 1937, the church is octagonal in shape to represent the eight Beatitudes that Matthew describes in his Gospel (Matthew 5: 3–10). Inscribed on each church window are the beginning words of one of the Beatitudes. A dome of glittery gold mosaic covers the altar and rests on top of the building. Surrounding the entire outside of the church are columned cloisters. These provide a beautiful, panoramic view of the Sea of Galilee.

20 We Go Forth in the Holy Spirit

 May God help us be strong in our faith.
May God bless us with peace.

Based on Psalm 29:11

Share

God's gifts are all around us. These gifts make us happy. We receive God's gifts through our five senses. Think about the good things that have happened to you this year. Write about them here.

Something beautiful I saw

_____

_____

_____

Something wonderful I heard

_____

_____

_____

Something nice I smelled

_____

_____

_____

Something delicious I tasted

_____

_____

_____

Something special I touched

_____

_____

_____

How can we praise God and bless other people?

✝ God's Grace and Blessing

One day God spoke to Moses. God said, "Moses, speak to your brother Aaron and to Aaron's sons. Tell them how I want them to **bless** others."

"All right," Moses answered. Then he told Aaron and his sons, "God wants you to bless other people. Pray for them and say, 'May God bless you and keep you safe! May God smile upon you. May he be generous with his love. May God look upon you kindly. May he always give you peace.'"

Based on Numbers 6:22–26

Signs of God's Love

A **blessing** is a sign of God's love for us. God told Moses how to give blessings to other people. The Holy Spirit helps us offer prayers of blessing to God. We bless God when we praise him and thank him for his gifts.

Our Church Teaches

When we bless God, we give him thanks and praise. When we ask God to bless others, we ask him to fill them with love and peace. When we ask God to bless ourselves, we ask for God's help through the Holy Spirit.

How can we share our blessings with others?

Respond

We Love and Serve

Each Mass ends with a blessing. The priest asks God to bless us. He reminds us to carry on the work of Jesus by helping, caring for, and serving others.

Priest: May almighty God bless you, the Father, and the Son, and the Holy Spirit.

All: Amen.

Priest: Go in peace to love and serve the Lord.

All: Thanks be to God.

The Order of Mass

WAYS TO LOVE AND SERVE OTHERS

We can be kind and patient.

We can cheerfully do chores and homework.

We can try to be helpful.

We can care for plants and animals.

We can share.

We can take part in parish activities.

We can ask God to bless others.

? How will you love and serve others this week?

Activities

1. Read the blessing prayer of Moses again.
   Complete each sentence. Use the missing words
   to complete the puzzle.

   > May God (3 down) you and keep you (5 across)!
   > May God (6 across) upon you.
   > May he be (1 down) with his love.
   > May God look upon you (4 across).
   > May he always give you (2 down).

   1 g

   2 p

   3 b

   4 i

   5 s

   6 s

2. Write your own prayer of blessing.

   _____
   -
   May God bless you and _____
   _____
   -
   _____ .

How can we
celebrate
God's
blessings?

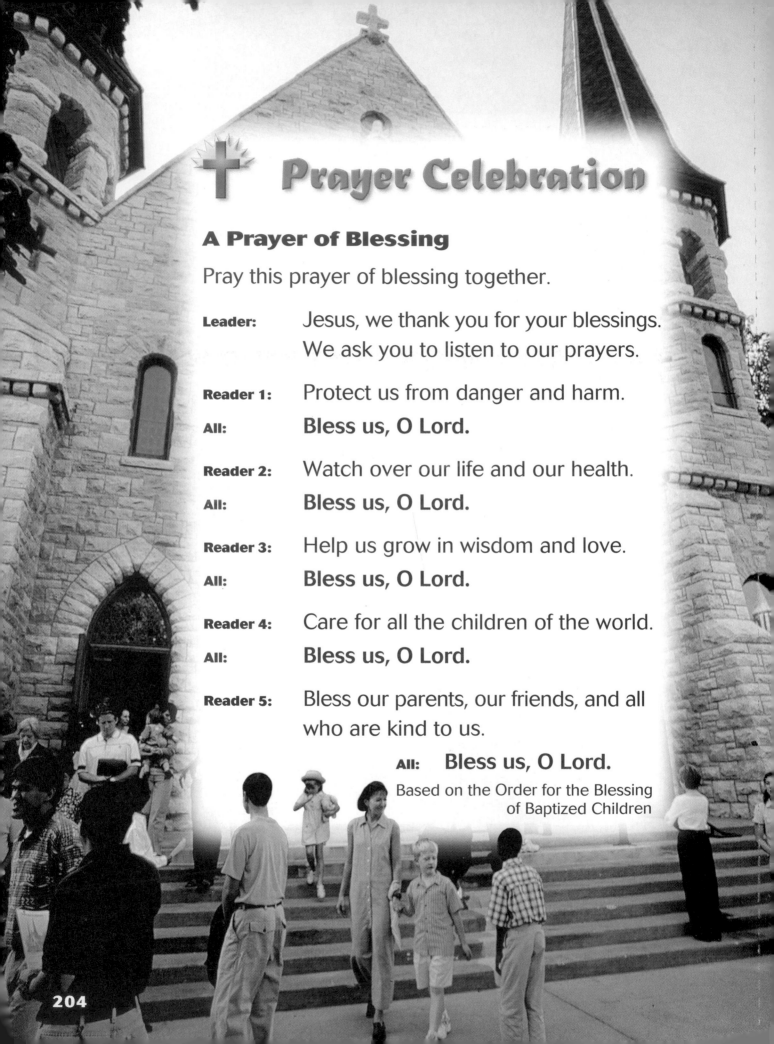

✝ Prayer Celebration

A Prayer of Blessing

Pray this prayer of blessing together.

Leader: Jesus, we thank you for your blessings. We ask you to listen to our prayers.

Reader 1: Protect us from danger and harm.

All: **Bless us, O Lord.**

Reader 2: Watch over our life and our health.

All: **Bless us, O Lord.**

Reader 3: Help us grow in wisdom and love.

All: **Bless us, O Lord.**

Reader 4: Care for all the children of the world.

All: **Bless us, O Lord.**

Reader 5: Bless our parents, our friends, and all who are kind to us.

All: **Bless us, O Lord.**

Based on the Order for the Blessing
of Baptized Children

WE CARE About the World

A Wise Law

Juan lives in a poor country called the Dominican Republic. His family is very poor. When Juan started school, he wore old, worn-out clothes. He did not have any shoes. Some children made fun of his clothes and his bare feet. They did not want to play with him. Juan did not like going to school.

Then a wise law was passed in Juan's country. All children had to wear school uniforms. The government helped poor families buy the uniforms. Everyone at school dressed alike. No one teased the poor children. All the children began to play together. Juan felt happy about going to school.

How did the wise law help the poor children?

Think About It

Some people choose their friends by the clothes they wear. Some people choose their friends by the color of their skin.

Learn About It

Jesus teaches us how to love other people. He does not want his followers to be prejudiced. The word prejudice means "to judge ahead of time." It means judging people by how they look on the outside. It means not giving a person a fair chance.

Do Something About It

All over the world, people who seem different are treated badly. What could you do to make friends with someone who seems different?
Add your ideas to the list.

Circle your answer for each question.

Do you think these are fair ways to choose a friend?

    yes   no

What really matters about a person?
    what is on the inside
    how a person looks

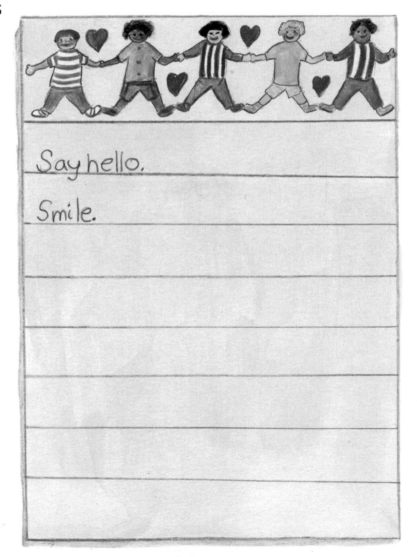

Say hello.

Smile.

Organizer

Connect the dots to find the picture.

Use the chapter titles to complete the sentences.

1 God gives us the _____ _____ _____ _____.

2 We celebrate _____ and service.

3 We work for peace and _____ _____.

4 We _____ _____ in the Holy Spirit.

A Use the letters in the box to complete the sentences. It will help if you cross out the letters as you use them.

g   f   s   a   J   r

1. Spiritual gifts help us follow ____ e s u s.

2. The Holy Spirit is our h e l p e ____.

3. Some spiritual gifts are k n o w l e d ____ e,

   w i ____ d o m, h e ____ l i n g, and ____ a i t h.

B Circle Yes or No.

1. All members of the Church are called to live in peace and serve others.   **Yes**   **No**

2. Baptized men and women may receive the sacrament of Matrimony.   **Yes**   **No**

3. All members of the Church serve God through the sacrament of Holy Orders.   **Yes**   **No**

4. Jesus wants us to get along with just a few people.   **Yes**   **No**

UNIT 5 Review

C Remember the story about the first followers of Jesus. Then circle the correct answer.

1. Early Christians were all of one heart and one ____.

   stomach   mind   song

2. They never let anyone go ____.

   home   outdoors   hungry

3. In the name of Christ Jesus, some of them gave food and ____.

   money   vacations   crayons

D Write the letter of the word that completes each sentence.

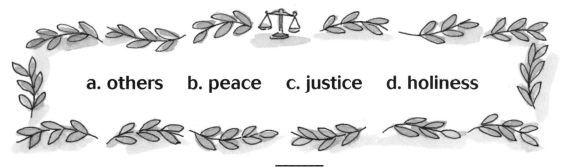

a. others   b. peace   c. justice   d. holiness

____
----
1. Jesus taught us to live in ____.

   ____
   ----
2. Jesus taught us to treat everyone with ____.

   ____
   ----
3. Peace means getting along with ____.

   ____
   ----
4. We grow in ____ when we make peace.

Review

E Remember the story "God's Grace and Blessing."
Use a ✔ to mark the sentences that are true.

☐ 1. God wanted Aaron and Aaron's sons to bless others.

☐ 2. Moses told Aaron to say, "May God be selfish with his love."

☐ 3. He told Aaron to say, "May God always give you peace."

F Draw a line under the word that completes each sentence.

1. God gives everyone his ____.
   Moses   blessing   name

2. A blessing is a prayer that praises ____.
   God   evil   trespasses

3. Each Mass ends with a ____.
   video   homily   blessing

4. The priest says, "Go in ____."
   anger   peace   worry

5. A blessing is a sign of ____.
   hate   love   summer

6. God wants us to bless ____.
   others   books   nobody

FEASTS AND SEASONS

The Liturgical Year

Holy Family
Epiphany
Baptism of the Lord

Christmas Time

Ordinary Time

Ash Wednesday

Christ the King

Advent

Lent

Passion Sunday (Palm Sunday)
Holy Thursday
Good Friday
Holy Saturday
Easter Sunday

Holy Week

Easter Time

Ascension

Pentecost

Trinity Sunday

The Body and Blood of Christ

Ordinary Time

December
25 Christmas Day
8 Immaculate Conception

January
1 Mary, Mother of God
25 Conversion of St. Paul

February
2 The Presentation
22 Chair of St. Peter

March
17 St. Patrick
19 St. Joseph
25 The Annunciation

November
1 All Saints' Day

October
4 St. Francis of Assisi
2 Guardian Angels

September

August
15 The Assumption

July

June
24 John the Baptizer

May
31 The Visitation

April

Advent

 Are you the one who is to come, or should we look for someone else?

Based on Matthew 11:3

Advent is the first season in the church year. During Advent we get ready for Jesus to come into our lives. We prepare our hearts for Jesus by being loving and caring.

Activity

This Advent house has windows with messages written on them. Each message tells one way we can prepare our hearts to welcome Jesus.

For each week of Advent, choose one window and follow its message.

Help a neighbor or a family member with a chore.

Give time or money to help someone in need.

Welcome a newcomer to your church or school.

Pray for someone who is unhappy.

Waiting for the Promised One

One Advent reading at Mass tells the story of John the Baptizer. He was an older cousin of Jesus. John went from town to town with a message. He said, "Make ready the way of the Lord." He wanted the people to prepare their hearts and minds for Jesus.

Based on Matthew 3:3

When Jesus began teaching, John sent a messenger to ask Jesus, "Are you the one for whom the people have been waiting for thousands of years?" Jesus answered, "Tell John that the blind see, the lame walk, the deaf hear, and the poor have heard the good news."

Based on Matthew 11:2–5

Hearing these words, John knew that Jesus was the Lord. The time of waiting was over.

Lord Jesus, come and save our world today. You have done great things for us. We are filled with joy.

Christmas

 The shepherds hurried to Bethlehem, where they found Mary and Joseph, and the infant Jesus lying in the manger.

Based on Luke 2:16

Signs of Christmas

Christmas is the season when we celebrate the birth of Jesus. If we look carefully, we will find signs of the Christmas story all around us.

Activity

Why do we have Christmas candy shaped like a shepherd's staff?

_____

_____

_____

_____

What does the star on the Christmas tree remind us of?

_____

_____

_____

_____

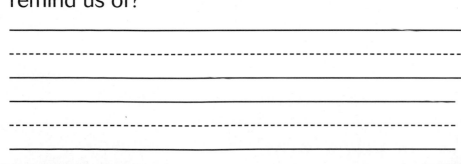

Telling the Christmas Story

Catholics love the Christmas story. We arrange figures into a lifelike display that retells the story. We call this display a crèche. This display is also called a nativity scene or a manger scene.

All during the Christmas season, we can visit the crèche in our church. When we do this, we think about the birth of Jesus. The figure of the Baby Jesus is put in the crèche on Christmas Day.

Long ago Saint Francis built the first crèche in Assisi, Italy. He built it outside and placed live animals in it. People came from far and near to pray at the crèche. By seeing the crèche, they learned the story of Jesus' birth in a way they would not forget.

Today in a manger is born our Savior, Jesus the Lord.

Lent

 Guide me in your ways, O Lord. Your path leads to your truth.

Based on Psalm 25:4–5

Marked with Jesus' Sign

At our baptism our parents and godparents marked us with the Sign of the Cross. The priest anointed the crown of our heads with oil in the Sign of the Cross.

At Mass we begin with the Sign of the Cross prayer. We end with the priest blessing us with the Sign of the Cross.

Activity

Decorate this cross with brightly colored markers or crayons. Think about what it means to belong to Jesus.

The First Day of Lent

Ash Wednesday is the first day of Lent. On this day we gather in church and are marked with ashes. The priest dips his thumb into the ashes. Then he traces the Sign of the Cross on our foreheads. Did you know that the first time you were marked with the Sign of the Cross was at your baptism? You were marked with Jesus' special sign. You became a member of Jesus' community, the Church.

Lent is a time to ask ourselves an important question. Are we living as members of Jesus' community should live? We could say that Lent is an "examination of conscience" for forty days. Each day you can ask yourself, "How can I be more loving in every way?"

Jesus, we are happy to belong to you. We are happy to be members of your community, the Church. Help us live each day as your followers. Amen.

Holy Week

Jesus said, "Take this bread and eat it. This is my Body. I give it to you."

Based on Matthew 26:26

Sharing a Special Meal

During Holy Week we celebrate three very holy days called the Easter Triduum. This is the most important time in the church year. The Triduum begins on Holy Thursday evening. At Mass we give thanks for the special meal that Jesus gave us.

Activity

Put a check (✓) on the line in front of the sentences that tell what happens at Mass.

_____ We sing songs.

_____ We pray the Our Father together.

_____ We receive Jesus in Holy Communion.

_____ We listen to readings from the Bible.

_____ The priest or deacon talks to us about the Gospel.

_____ We wish one another peace.

Add a sentence of your own.

_____

_____

_____

Three Holy Days

On the day before Jesus died on the cross, he shared a special meal with his followers. He did this to show his love and concern for them. We remember the Last Supper on Holy Thursday evening.

Jesus shares the same special meal with us today. We call this meal the Eucharist. The word Eucharist means "thanksgiving." Jesus is with us in a special way in the Eucharist. Jesus gives us himself in Holy Communion.

Good Friday is another holy day. On Good Friday we remember the day that Jesus died on the cross. We remember that Jesus died so that we can have new life.

On the night of Holy Saturday we celebrate Jesus' rising to new life. We begin our Easter celebration.

Jesus,
thank you for giving yourself to us in the Eucharist.
Amen.

Easter

I have seen Jesus! He is alive!

Based on John 20:18

Words of Joy

We can show we are happy and filled with joy in many ways. Sometimes we sing. Sometimes we dance. Sometimes we even shout and jump up and down. We might even give someone a great big hug!

We also show our joy in the words we use. These words let others know just how happy we are.

Activity

Circle the words below that you might use to show you are filled with joy.

Alleluia! Jesus Is Risen!

Easter is our most important feast. On Easter we celebrate the good news that Jesus is not dead. Jesus is alive! He is with us today!

Our parish community gathers at Mass. We sing songs filled with joy. We pray prayers of thanksgiving. We thank God for the new life he gave to Jesus and shares with us. We receive Holy Communion.

We use the word <u>Alleluia</u> to tell about our deep joy. Alleluia is our Easter word of joy and peace. When we came together during Lent, our church community did not pray or sing, "Alleluia." But now it is Easter, and we listen to the word of God that proclaims Jesus' new life. We are happy and filled with God's joy. We pray and sing, "Alleluia!"

Jesus,
you are risen
from the dead.
Alleluia! Alleluia!
Amen.

Holy Days

People will know that you are my friends, if you love one another.

Based on John 13:35

What's in a Name?

Every person has a name that is special to him or her. Our names tell some interesting things about us.

Jovito

Activity

What is your name?

GISELA

_____

- -

_____

Why did your parents give you that name?

Roger

Check (✓) the reasons below that are true for you.

_____ I was given the same name as my mom or dad and am proud to have it.

SIOK-TIN

_____ I was given my name to honor my grandparent or another family member.

_____ I was named after a good friend of my mother's or father's.

Thomas

_____ My parents really loved my name and wanted me to have it.

Cleora

_____ I was given the name of an outstanding person in my community or country.

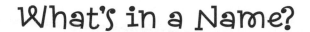

All Saints' Day

Among Catholics it has long been a custom to name our children for saints. Saints are those who live outstanding lives as followers of Jesus. Saints put all their energy into doing what is good. They use the strength of their spirit to fight what is bad.

Francis of Assisi is one saint whom we honor. He gave up money, parties, and fancy clothes. Instead he spent his time in prayer and joyful love of all God's creatures.

The Church names many people as saints. Each saint can help us learn more about how to be true

followers of Jesus. We can ask the saints in prayer for help to lead good Christian lives. We can ask for their prayers for fairness for all people and for peace among people.

We celebrate the Feast of All Saints on November 1.

All holy men and women, pray for us that we may live more like Jesus. Amen.

Mary

Hail, Mary, full of grace. The Lord is with you.

Based on Luke 1:28

The Hail Mary

Our Church honors the saints with our prayers. Our greatest saint is Mary. The prayer we use most often as a church community to honor Mary is the Hail Mary.

Activity

Pray the words of the Hail Mary slowly. Fill in the missing words.

Hail Mary, full of __grace__,

the Lord is with you.

Blessed are you among women,

and __blessed__ is the fruit of your

womb, Jesus.

Holy Mary, __mother__ of God,

pray for us sinners, now,

and at the hour of our death. __Amen__

A Prayer to Honor Mary

God's angel asked Mary to be the mother of God's own Son. The angel greeted Mary with these words, "Hail, Mary, full of grace. The Lord is with you." Later Mary went to see Elizabeth, her cousin. Elizabeth greeted Mary by saying, "Blessed are you among women, and blessed is the fruit of your womb, Jesus."

Based on Luke 1:26–42

Do these words sound familiar to you? These same words can be found in the Hail Mary. We pray the Hail Mary to honor Mary, the Mother of God. We ask Mary to pray for us now and when it is our time to go home to God. We know that Mary loves us like a mother and prays for us always.

Hail Mary, our mother, pray for us now and at the hour of our death. Amen.

Saints

Blessed are the poor in spirit.

Matthew 5:3

Service to Others

Jesus came to teach us how to serve one another. He showed us how to help people. Can you think of some ways that Jesus served others in need?

Activity

This picture story shows Jesus getting ready to serve others. It also shows some hungry people.

Write a title for the picture story on the line.

_____

- -

_____

Saint Margaret of Scotland

Margaret of Scotland was a queen. She was married to Malcolm, the king of Scotland. They were very rich and could have lived selfish lives. But Queen Margaret was not happy keeping all the riches for herself. So she and the king shared their money and food with the poor people of their country. They gave slaves their freedom. They cared for everyone who needed their love.

Queen Margaret prayed every day. She read the Bible and taught her children to love God. She also taught them to care for people in need. Margaret chose to live as Jesus lived.

In time, Margaret became the patron saint of Scotland. Today we honor Saint Margaret for her service to God's people. She is a Christian hero. November 16 is the feast of Saint Margaret.

> Saint Margaret of Scotland, pray with us for all those people who are in need today. Amen.

Holy People

See what love the Father has poured out on us. We are called God's children.

Based on 1 John 3:1

The Same but Different

Annie knows she looks like her mom. But Annie acts more like her dad. And in some ways, Annie is like no one else. She is special!

Michael is adopted. He doesn't look like anyone in his family. But Michael is like his family members in other ways. He is kind. He has a good sense of humor and likes to laugh.

Maybe you look like another family member. Maybe you don't. Maybe you act like your older brother or sister. Or maybe you just act like yourself. But there is one way in which you are just like everyone else. You are a child of God! And that makes you and everyone else very special!

Activity

Complete the sentence below.

I am special because

Dr. Martin Luther King Jr.

Dr. Martin Luther King Jr. grew up in the large city of Atlanta, Georgia. There his father was a minister in the Baptist Church. Martin studied hard at school and went to college. He became a minister, too.

When Martin was a grown man, he began his important work. He wanted all people to have the food they needed to be healthy. He wanted everyone to be treated with respect and fairness. Dr. King marched in the streets of Atlanta and other cities for the rights of all people. As a leader, he gave powerful speeches. He prayed. He preached the good news of Jesus.

Not everyone liked what Dr. King was saying and doing. His words made some people feel angry and afraid. In 1968, Dr. King was killed.

Dr. Martin Luther King Jr. was a special follower of Jesus. Our country honors him by celebrating his birthday in January.

Martin Luther King Jr., you gave us an example of how to live Jesus' Good News that we are God's children. Pray for us that we might follow in your footsteps. Amen.

OUR CATHOLIC HERITAGE

WHAT CATHOLICS BELIEVE

We can come to know and understand our faith in many ways.

ABOUT
THE BIBLE

The <u>Bible</u> is the word of God. In the Bible there are many books written by different people. God especially chose each writer. And each writer tells stories about God's love for us.

The Bible is also called Scripture. <u>Scripture</u> means "holy writings."

The Bible has two parts—the Old Testament and the New Testament. At Mass there are readings from both parts of the Bible.

The Old Testament is about God's people who lived before Jesus was born.

The New Testament is about Jesus' life and his teachings. It includes important books and letters for the followers of Jesus.

The first four books in the New Testament are called Gospels. <u>Gospel</u> means "good news." The Gospels are named for four of Jesus' disciples—Matthew, Mark, Luke, and John. Each Gospel tells us good news about Jesus.

DO YOU KNOW THESE STORIES FROM THE BIBLE?

ABOUT
THE TRINITY

There is only one God. There are three Persons in God—the Father, the Son, and the Holy Spirit.

We call the three Persons in God the Holy Trinity.

The Nicene Creed tells about the Holy Trinity. The words tell what we believe about God the Father, Son, and Holy Spirit.

God Our Father

God is our heavenly Father. Like a good father, God loves and cares for us. When Jesus taught us to pray, he told us to call God "Father." God is also our Creator. And God made everything in the world with love.

Jesus Christ

Jesus Christ is God's own Son. Jesus became a man and lived on the earth. God sent Jesus to teach us.

Jesus teaches us about God. He teaches us how to live as children of God. And he teaches us how to show love. When we do these things, we are followers of Jesus.

Jesus died on the cross and rose from the dead for us. Jesus is our Savior. He saves us from sin. And he saves us from death.

Jesus is alive. He shares new life with us.

The Holy Spirit

The Holy Spirit is God. The Holy Spirit is always with us. The Holy Spirit helps us follow Jesus.

We receive the Holy Spirit at Baptism. The Holy Spirit gives us gifts that help us live good lives. We can share these gifts with other people and with the Church. The Holy Spirit helps us live as Jesus teaches us to live.

ABOUT
THE CATHOLIC CHURCH

We are Catholics. We are God's people. We call the Church the Body of Christ. We are followers of Jesus. We celebrate the sacraments. We pray to God. We can pray together or by ourselves. We care for and help others.

The Catholic Church is our faith community. Our church community shares the good news about Jesus.

MARY

Mary is the mother of Jesus. She was chosen by God.

Mary loved and trusted God. Mary loved and cared for Jesus.

We call Mary "Mother," too. She is our mother in heaven. Like a good mother, Mary loves and cares for us. Mary hears our prayers.

Mary is our greatest saint. The saints are special people. Saints show us how to follow Jesus. We honor Mary and all the saints. We ask them to pray for us.

ABOUT

NEW LIFE FOREVER

Jesus teaches us to act with love. When we act with love, we will be happy with God in heaven. Heaven is happiness with God forever.

HOW CATHOLICS WORSHIP

Worship is giving honor, thanks, and praise to God. We worship when we pray and when we celebrate the Eucharist. We worship when we celebrate all the sacraments.

ABOUT
THE SACRAMENTS

The sacraments are celebrations of God's love for us. We celebrate that we belong to Jesus. We celebrate that we share in Jesus' new life. There are seven sacraments.

Baptism is a sacrament of welcome into the Church. At Baptism we receive the Holy Spirit. We are baptized with water. Water is a sign that Jesus shares his new life with us.

Confirmation is the sacrament of the Holy Spirit. In Confirmation we receive the Holy Spirit in a special way. The Holy Spirit helps us share the good news about Jesus.

Eucharist is the sacrament in which we share a special meal with Jesus. The Eucharist, a sacrifice, is God's gift to us.

When we celebrate the Eucharist at Mass, we remember that Jesus loves us. Jesus saves us from sin and gives us everlasting life. We thank God for giving us the Body and Blood of Jesus Christ to make us his people.

Reconciliation is the sacrament that celebrates the gift of God's forgiveness. It also celebrates the gift of God's love for us. We say we are sorry for our sins. We promise to turn away from sin. God always forgives us.

Anointing of the Sick is a sacrament of healing. It is the sacrament of Jesus' peace and forgiveness. People who are sick or elderly receive this sacrament.

The sacrament of **Holy Orders** celebrates priests, deacons, and bishops. These people are called by God to do Jesus' work in the Church.

Matrimony is the sacrament that celebrates the love that a man and a woman have for each other. In marriage a husband and wife begin their own family. Together with their children they can be models for the whole community. They can show others what it means to follow Jesus.

ABOUT
THE MASS

1. Our celebration begins. The priest and the other ministers go to the altar. We stand and sing a welcome song.

2. We make the Sign of the Cross. The priest welcomes us with these words: "The Lord be with you." We answer, "And also with you."

3. We remember our sins. We ask God to forgive us.

4. We listen to God's word in two readings from the Bible. At the end of each reading we say, "Thanks be to God."

5. The priest or deacon reads the Gospel story. The word <u>Gospel</u> means "good news." We stand and listen to the good news of Jesus. We say, "Praise to you, Lord Jesus Christ."

6. The priest or deacon explains the readings to us in a special talk called the homily. We listen carefully.

7. We stand and pray the Prayer of the Faithful. We ask God to help the Church, our country, and all of God's people.

8. We bring the gifts of bread and wine to the altar for the special meal with Jesus. We remember that Jesus always loves us.

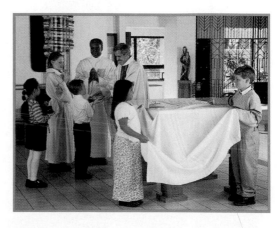

9. The priest offers our gifts of bread and wine to God.

10. We thank and praise God for all of our blessings. We especially thank God for the gift of Jesus.

11. The priest prays as Jesus did at the Last Supper. Our gifts of bread and wine become the Body and Blood of Jesus Christ.

12. The priest holds up the Body and Blood of Jesus. He says a prayer to praise God. We answer, "Amen." The word Amen means "Yes! We believe this is true."

13. We say the Lord's Prayer. This is the prayer that Jesus taught us to say.

14. We offer one another a Sign of Peace. This is a sign that reminds us to live as Jesus teaches us to live.

15. When we share Jesus' Body and Blood in the Eucharist, we promise to act like Jesus.

16. We receive God's blessing. We answer, "Amen." Together we sing a communion song that gives thanks and praise for the gift of Jesus in the Eucharist. We go in peace to love and serve all people.

ABOUT
RECONCILIATION

The sacrament of Reconciliation is a celebration of God's love and forgiveness. We can celebrate the sacrament of Reconciliation with others.

Introductory Rites We sing a song of praise. The priest welcomes us and prays with us.

The Word of God We listen to readings from the Bible. The priest or deacon helps us understand the readings.

Examination of Conscience We think about our words and actions. We ask the Holy Spirit to help us turn away from sin. We pray the Lord's Prayer together.

Rite of Reconciliation We pray a prayer of sorrow. Then each of us tells our sins to the priest. We talk about the words or actions for which we are sorry. Then we ask for forgiveness. The priest gives us absolution—the forgiveness of God.

Proclamation of Praise We praise and thank God. We are happy that God forgives us. We are happy that he loves us always and forever.

Concluding Prayer of Thanksgiving The priest offers a blessing for us. We sing a song of praise.

Steps to Reconciliation

When we receive the sacrament of Reconciliation, we follow these steps:

1. **Examination of Conscience** I examine my conscience. I ask myself some important questions. Have I hurt other people or myself? Have I done harmful things on purpose?

2. **Welcome** The priest offers a welcome. I make the Sign of the Cross and say, "In the name of the Father, and of the Son, and of the Holy Spirit. Amen."

3. **Reading** The priest may read a story from the Bible. The story is about God's love and forgiveness. God is always ready to forgive.

4. **Confession of Sins** The priest listens as I talk. I explain my sins. I tell the priest how I may have hurt myself or others.

5. **Penance** The priest asks me to say a prayer or do an act of goodness. This will help me make up for what I have done wrong.

6. Prayer of Sorrow I tell God I am sorry for my sins. I say a prayer of sorrow. This prayer is called the Act of Contrition.

> My God,
> I am sorry for my sins with all my heart.
> In choosing to do wrong
> and failing to do good,
> I have sinned against you
> whom I should love above all things.
> I firmly intend, with your help,
> to do penance,
> to sin no more,
> and to avoid whatever leads me to sin.
> Amen.

7. Absolution The priest says a prayer in the name of the Church. Then the priest asks God to forgive my sins. The priest gives me absolution, which is the forgiveness of God.

The priest says, "I absolve you from your sins in the name of the Father, and of the Son, and of the Holy Spirit."

8. Prayer of Praise and Dismissal With the priest, I thank God for being forgiving. This is called the Prayer of Thanksgiving. Then the priest says, "Go in peace."

I answer, "Amen."

HOW CATHOLICS LIVE

Jesus teaches us how to live.
He gives us the Holy Spirit to help us.
He gives us the sacraments in the Church
to strengthen us in doing good.

THE GREAT COMMANDMENT

Jesus told us that all of God's Commandments are really one Great Commandment. Jesus said, "You must love God with all your heart, all your thoughts, and all your strength. You must love your neighbor as yourself" (based on Mark 12:30–31; Deuteronomy 6:5).

The Great Commandment tells us how to love God and other people.

ABOUT
THE NEW COMMANDMENT

Jesus gave us the New Commandment. He said, "Love one another as I have loved you." (based on John 13:34)

We can show our love by caring for all living things. We can be fair and kind to all people. We can be helpful. We can be forgiving. We can be peacemakers.

When we do not treat others with love, we sin. Sin is turning away from God and choosing to do what we know is wrong. God wants us to be sorry for our sins. God always forgives us. God wants us always to be loving people.

The Holy Spirit Helps Us

We can make the choice to love or to sin. The Holy Spirit helps us turn away from sin and choose what is good.

ABOUT
THE BEATITUDES

The Bible tells us a story of Jesus as a great teacher. The story is called "The Sermon on the Mount." This story tells us about the lesson that Jesus taught his followers. He taught them about the eight Beatitudes. The Beatitudes tell us how to live and how to treat others.

The Beatitudes	Living the Beatitudes
Happy are the poor in spirit. The reign of God is theirs.	We are poor in spirit when we know that we need God more than anything else.
Happy are the sorrowful. They will be comforted.	We try to help those who are in sorrow or those who are hurting. We know God will comfort them.
Happy are the gentle. They will receive all that God has promised.	We are gentle and patient with others. We believe we will share in God's promises.
Happy are those who hunger and thirst for justice. They will be satisfied.	We try to be fair and just toward others. We share what we have with those in need.
Happy are those who show mercy. They will receive mercy.	We forgive those who are unkind to us. We accept the forgiveness of others.
Happy are the pure of heart. They will see God.	We try to keep God first in our lives. We believe we will live forever with God.
Happy are the peacemakers. They will be called the children of God.	We try to bring God's peace to the world. When we live peacefully, we are known as God's children.
Happy are those who are treated unfairly for doing what is right. The kingdom of heaven will belong to them.	We try to do what is right even when we are teased or insulted. We believe we will be with God forever.

ABOUT
THE TEN COMMANDMENTS

We can find God's commandments in the Bible. The Ten Commandments tell us how God wants us to live. When we live by the commandments, we grow in holiness.

The Ten Commandments
We Live God's Laws

We believe that there is only one God.

We respect the name of God.

We go to Mass on Sunday.

We respect our parents.

We take care of all that God has made.

We treat our bodies as a gift from God.

We respect the property of others.

We always tell the truth.

We respect the families of others.

We are content with what we have.

ABOUT
VOCATIONS

When we were baptized, we became members of the Catholic community. God calls each of us to live our lives in a special way. This is called our <u>vocation</u>.

God calls some people to a religious vocation. This is a call to a special way of life in the Church. Priests, religious sisters, and other clergy have a religious vocation.

Many Ways of Helping

God calls Catholics to help in many different ways.

Catholics can help at Mass by reading the Bible, leading songs, or giving Holy Communion to people.

Catholics can teach others about God. They can teach Jesus' Gospel message.

Catholics can visit sick people who need help. Catholics can teach in schools.

Catholics who share the good news about Jesus' love are answering God's call.

God calls some people to help the Church in a special way. Priests do the work of Jesus by saying Mass, celebrating the sacraments, and leading the parish community.

Some religious sisters and brothers teach. Other religious sisters and brothers help the poor. Others serve as parish leaders.

Deacons help our priest in many ways. At Mass they can read the Gospel or give the homily. Deacons can celebrate the sacraments of Baptism and Matrimony. They also help people who are in need.

As you get older, God will call you to serve him in your Catholic community. You might read the Bible at Mass. You might be a teacher. Perhaps God will call you to a religious vocation.

ABOUT
RELIGIOUS SISTERS

Religious sisters have a special vocation. They belong to groups called communities. They spend their lives working for God and for all of God's people.

Some sisters teach in elementary schools, high schools, and colleges. Some sisters work among the poor, the sick, and the elderly. Still others are missioners. They bring the good news of the Gospel to people in countries all over the world.

Each religious sister makes important promises. She promises God that she will love him. She promises that she will live a simple life. She promises to be an example of what is good. She promises to be an example of a good Christian life.

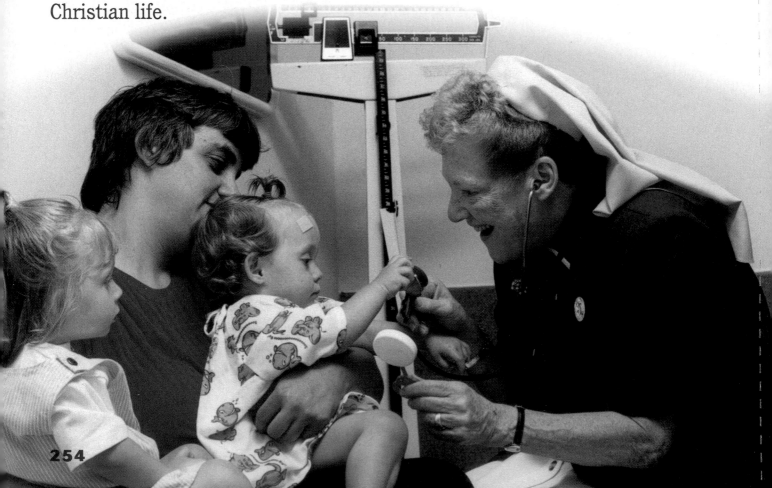

HOW CATHOLICS PRAY

Prayer is talking and listening to God. We can pray anywhere and at any time. God is everywhere. God always hears our prayers.

ABOUT
KINDS OF PRAYER

When we pray, we spend time with God. We need to pray every day.

Everyone can pray. There are many different reasons why we pray.

We can pray for someone we love. We can say a prayer to praise God. We can say a prayer of sorrow to God. We can pray just to share our thoughts with God. We can say, "I love you, God." We can pray to say, "Thank you, God."

We can pray with others, as we do at Mass. We can pray by saying a prayer quietly in our hearts. We can pray by sitting very still. We can just listen to the sounds around us.

A dance, a song, and a smile can all be a special prayer. If our hearts are filled with love, then our actions become special prayers.

ABOUT
THE LORD'S PRAYER

The Lord's Prayer is a very special prayer. Jesus taught us the words to say.

In this prayer Jesus teaches us to call God "Our Father." In this prayer we honor God. We pray that what God wants for us will be done. We ask God for what we need. We ask God to keep us safe. Then we say, "Amen."

The Lord's Prayer

Our Father, who art in heaven, hallowed be thy name;
God is our Father. We praise God.
We pray that everyone will say God's name with love.

thy kingdom come;
Jesus told us about God's kingdom. God's kingdom is happiness with God forever.
We pray that everyone in the world will know God's love.

thy will be done on earth as it is in heaven.
We pray that everyone will live in peace. We pray that everyone will follow God's word.

Give us this day our daily bread;
God is good. God cares for us. We pray for our needs and for the needs of others.

and forgive us our trespasses as we forgive those who trespass against us;
We ask God to forgive us when we sin. We remember that we must forgive others, too.

and lead us not into temptation,
We pray that God will help us make good choices.

but deliver us from evil.
We pray that God will protect us from things that may harm us.

Amen.
Our "Amen" says that Jesus' prayer is our prayer, too.

Write-In Glossary

absolution

_____

- -

_____ is the forgiveness of God given through the priest in the sacrament of Reconciliation.

act of contrition

_____

- -

An _____ is a prayer that tells God we are sorry for our sins. We make up our minds not to sin again.

Anointing of the Sick

_____   _____

- - - - - - - - - - - - - - - - -   - - - - - - - - - - -

_____ **of the** _____ is a sacrament that brings peace and the forgiveness of Christ to people who are sick or elderly.

Baptism

_____

- -

In the sacrament of _____ the Church welcomes us as new members. Baptism takes away original sin and all other sin. The Holy Spirit comes to us in Baptism.

Bible

_____

- -

The _____ is the word of God. It tells about the love God has for us. It is also called the Scriptures.

bless

_____

- - - - - - - - - - - - - - - - - - - -

_____ means to ask for God's good will toward someone.

blessing A _____ is a prayer that praises God. A blessing asks for God's gifts for others or for ourselves.

Body of Christ The Catholic Church is the _____ _____.

confession _____ is telling our sins to a priest in the sacrament of Reconciliation.

Confirmation In the sacrament of _____ we receive strength to follow Jesus.

conscience Our _____ helps us know right from wrong.

contrition _____ means to be sorry and to want to stay away from sin.

Eucharist The sacrament of _____ is a sacrifice and a special meal of thanks. In the Eucharist, God gives us the Body and Blood of Christ.

free choice　　_____ is the freedom
God gives us to choose between right and wrong.

Gospel　　The word _____ means "good
news." The four Gospels are books in the Bible that tell the
good news of Jesus' life and teachings.

grace　　The gift of God's _____ helps us stay
away from sin. Grace is God's loving presence in our lives.

Great Commandment　　The _____ _____
is "You must love God with all your heart, all your thoughts,
and all your strength. Love your neighbor as yourself."

hallowed　　_____ is another word
for "holy."

heaven　　_____ is happiness with
God forever.

holy

_____

- - - - - - - - - - - - - - -

To be _____ means to be like God. Holy people act like Jesus.

Holy Communion

We receive the Body and Blood of Christ in _____

- -

_____.

Holy Orders

_____

- -

_____ is a sacrament of service. God calls some men to serve the Church as deacons, priests, and bishops.

homily

_____

- -

A _____ is a talk given by a priest or deacon. It explains the Bible readings we have heard at Mass.

justice

_____

- -

_____ means treating people as they deserve to be treated.

Liturgy of the Eucharist

_____   _____

- - - - - - - - - - - - -   -

The _____ **of the** _____ begins as we prepare to share a special meal with Jesus.

Liturgy of the Word

_____   _____

- - - - - - - - - - - - - - - -   - - - - - - - - - - - - - - - -

The _____ **of the** _____ is the part of Mass when we listen to readings from the Bible.

Matrimony

_____ is a sacrament of service. God calls husbands and wives to love one another and form a Christian family.

mortal sin

A _____ is a serious sin that separates us from our friendship with God.

New Commandment

The _____ _____ is "Love one another as I have loved you."

Nicene Creed

Catholics tell what they believe when they pray the _____ _____ at Mass. The creed tells about God's love for us and about how Jesus saved us.

original sin

_____ is the sin of the first people on the earth. Because we are born with original sin, it is harder for us to do what is right.

peace

_____ is not fighting. It means getting along with others.

penance

A _____ is a prayer or kind act to make up for doing wrong.

praise

_____

_____ is a joyful type of prayer. It celebrates God's goodness.

prayer

_____

_____ is talking to and listening to God.

Prayer of the Faithful

The _____ **of the** _____ is the last part of the Liturgy of the Word at Mass. During this prayer we pray for ourselves and for people everywhere.

Reconciliation

_____ is a sacrament of healing that celebrates God's love and forgiveness.

Resurrection

_____ is Jesus' being raised from the dead to new life.

sacrament

A _____ is a special celebration of the Church. The sacraments are signs that God is here with us now.

sacraments of initiation

There are three _____ _____. In Baptism we become members of the Church. In Confirmation we receive strength to follow Jesus. In Eucharist we share a special meal with Jesus.

sacrifice   A _____ is a special gift that is given out of love.

saint   A _____ is a person who shows great love for other people and for God.

Savior   A _____ is someone who rescues others from danger. Jesus is our Savior. He saves us from sin and death.

Scripture   The Bible is also called _____. Scripture means "Holy Writings."

service   _____ means doing work that helps others.

sin   We _____ when we choose to hurt others and turn away from God.

Son of God   _____ is a special title for Jesus. Jesus is human, like us. Jesus is also God's Son.

spiritual gifts   The _____ help us follow Jesus. Some of these gifts are knowledge, wisdom, healing, and faith.

temptation
A _____ is a feeling of wanting to do something that is wrong.

Ten Commandments
The _____ are God's laws. They teach us how to love God, others, and ourselves.

trespasses
_____ are sins or wrongs we do on purpose. Trespasses separate us from God and other people.

venial sin
A _____ is a less serious sin than a mortal sin. It weakens our friendship with God, but it does not take it away.

vocation
A _____ is God's call to us to live our lives in a special way.

word of God
The _____ is another name for the Bible.

works of mercy
The _____ tell how Jesus wants us to help others.

Index

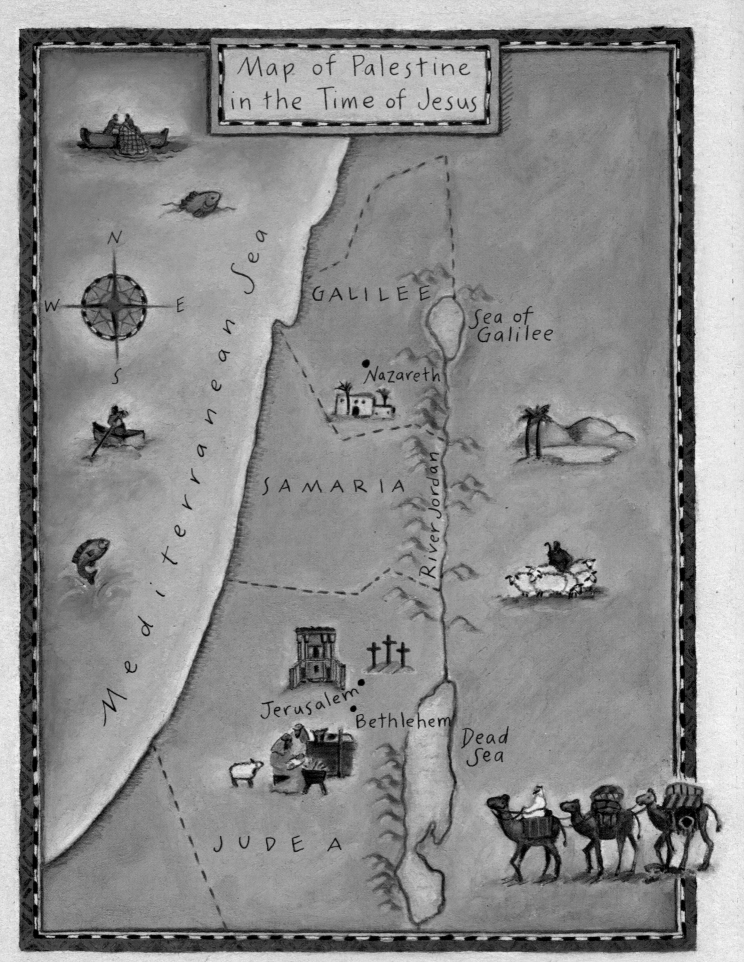